Jacqueline Tobin is the author of *The Tao Women*, and is also a teacher, collector, and writer of women's stories. She lives in Denver, Colorado. Raymond Dobard, Ph.D., is an art history professor at Howard University and a nationally known African American quilter. He lives in Washington, D.C.

HIDDEN IN

PLAIN VIEW

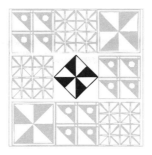

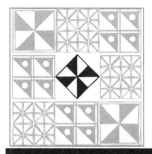
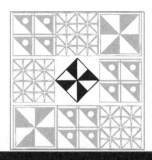

Jacqueline L. Tobin
and
Raymond G. Dobard, Ph.D.

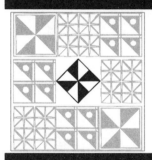

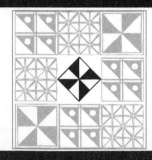

ANCHOR BOOKS
A Division of Random House, Inc.
New York

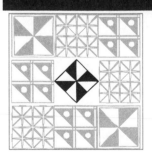
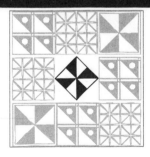

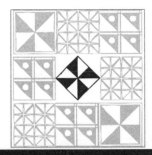
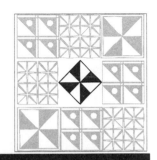

HIDDEN IN PLAIN VIEW

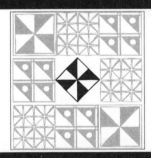
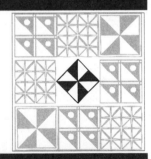

A SECRET STORY
OF QUILTS AND THE
UNDERGROUND RAILROAD

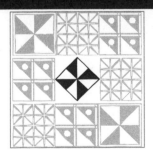
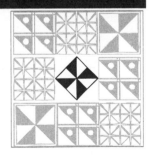

FIRST ANCHOR BOOKS EDITION, JANUARY 2000

The Library of Congress has cataloged the Doubleday edition as follows:
Tobin, Jacqueline, 1950–
Hidden in plain view / Jacqueline L. Tobin and Raymond G. Dobard
—1st ed.
p.   cm.
Includes bibliographical references.
1. Underground railroad.   2. Fugitive slaves—United States—
Communication—History—19th century.   3. Afro-American quilts—
Social aspects—History—19th century.   4. Ciphers—History—19th
century.   I. Dobard, Raymond G.   II. Title.
E450.T63   1999
973.7'115—dc21   98-49804
CIP

ISBN 0-385-49767-9

www.anchorbooks.com

Printed in the United States of America
10   9   8   7   6   5   4   3   2   1

We dedicate this book to Ozella McDaniel Williams,
to her mother Nora Bell McDaniel, and to her grandmother before her,
for keeping the Underground Railroad Quilt story alive.
And to the memory of everyone who struggled for freedom,
but whose stories have yet to be told.

ACKNOWLEDGMENTS

From Jacqueline L. Tobin

When Ozella McDaniel Williams first told me to "write this down," little did I know that she was introducing me to a network of people dedicated to keeping African American history alive. Many of these people have contributed to this book; I am indebted to them all. Persons such as Prince Hall Mason historian Joseph Walkes, Jr., who generously shared his research with me; Elizabeth and Joyce Scott, who described to me the African retentions and personal memories stitched in their quilts and fabric art; the people of the Buxton Township Museum in North Buxton, Ontario, who sent me pictures of slave-made quilts; Deborah Hopkinson and James Ransome, who readily returned letters and phone calls and encouraged me with the story and pictures in their book *Sweet Clara and the Freedom Quilt*; Arthur Jones, who taught me a great deal and soothed me with his renditions of the spirituals; and Amy Blyth of the Charleston Convention and Visitors Bureau for her support in connecting me to the history of her city.

Stewart, you never questioned my passion for this story and have always supported me in ways that allowed me to follow its threads, wherever it took me. I thank you. B.J., you have been my companion on these sojourns in search of quilters and their stories. You are the keeper of the stories in our family; we are indebted to you. And to my children, Alex and Jasmine, who tolerated my absences and lack of attention, this book is also a gift to you. May you never lack for the stories of your ancestors.

And, finally, to my friend and coauthor Raymond Dobard, for his belief in me and for agreeing to share this journey. Thank you.

Ozella, I stand humbly in front of the mirror, surrounded by your quilts and wisdom. Thank you for entrusting me with your story. I hope this book honors you.

From Raymond G. Dobard

When I said yes to coauthoring this book with Jacki, little did I know how much of my life would be consumed by the story of Mrs. Ozella McDaniel Williams, her intriguing Underground Railroad Quilt Code, quilt patterns, African art and culture, the history of slavery, and African American history. The research and writing of *Hidden in Plain View* triggered childhood memories of New Orleans and the cultural patchwork of races and religious beliefs that belonged to my African American Creole heritage. I found myself remembering people and customs I'd known well, especially the importance of secrets within the black community. Coauthoring *Hidden in Plain View* enabled me to add to the compelling history of the Underground Railroad. For this opportunity I thank Mrs. Ozella McDaniel Williams and Jacqueline L. Tobin, my coauthor, who invited me to join her in honoring Ozella's story.

I wish to acknowledge the many people who became intensely involved in Ozella's story: from the staff of the Moorland-Spingarn Research Center at Howard University, whose professionalism and human interest were exceptional; to the patience of Saba Cla Williams, a Howard University student, who was the first person to assist me in researching material on the Prince Hall Masons; to my Departmental Chairman, Dr. Floyd Coleman, for his unwavering encouragement; to Mrs. Cuesta R. Benberry, a pioneer in the field of quilt scholarship, who was a mentor and was *always there* with her encyclopedic knowledge of quilt history; and to Mr. Christian Harrison, a student of design in the Department of Art at Howard University, who generously gave of his talent and time to illustrate the Underground Railroad map.

I express a debt of gratitude to friends and associates like Dr. Leslie King-Hammond, who shared her insight on the work of Mrs. Elizabeth T. Scott and the *lukasa* tradition; Mrs. Elizabeth T. Scott, who gave of her talent; Ms. Joyce Scott, who remembered her mother's stories; Dr.

Robert Cargo for allowing access to his wonderful quilt collection; Dr. Mary Nooter, who helped secure the *lukasa* image and whose work on African art inspired us; and Mr. Leland Beers of Dresden, Ohio, who took me on a phone tour of his city and described its Underground Railroad station.

The acknowledgments would be incomplete without a special mention of Yawa Book and Gift Shop of Washington, D.C. The name *Yawa* is an African term of the Hausa people and means "abundance." Not only was I to find an abundance of books and knowledge at Yawa, but also another Hausa tradition defined by the word *dakasuwa*. *Dakasuwa*, which translates as marketplace, refers to the friendly spirit and exchange of goods, ideas, and caring that is traditional to the African marketplace. Mr. Magaji Bukar, the owner, and his son Mr. Darrell C. Hawkins were there for both Jacki and me from the very beginning of our work. At Yawa, I quickly found what became my place of refuge while writing this book, a spot in front of a window that looked onto the alley and was adjacent to shelves of books on African art and African American culture. For nearly two years that one spot in front of a window invited me to take books from Yawa's shelves and to read in a soft quiet light. There I would enjoy solace from a noisy, crowded world. Yawa was my "safe house" on this publishing journey and for that I am most grateful.

To my friends and relatives, who tolerated my absence and my obsessive behavior while writing this book, I thank you for your patience, your support, and your love.

From the Authors

We are indebted to the scholarship and wisdom of Cuesta Benberry, Floyd Coleman, Ph.D., and Maude Wahlman, Ph.D., without whom this book could not have been written. From the beginning, they recognized the value of the story. To our agent, Madeline Morel, and our editor, Janet Hill (whose insight guided us), we are grateful because they understood the importance of sharing the story with the world. To the Doubleday team we never met, but who supported us behind the scenes: Copy Editing, Production, Design, Cover Art, Publicity, Marketing, and Sales—and to Deputy Publisher Michael Palgon—thank you one and all. We were privileged to have taken the Gullah Tour with Alphonso Brown, who gave us the African American perspective on the history of Charleston and introduced us to the venerable blacksmith Philip Simmons. We are appreciative to the following museums and collections for providing photographs for publication: The National Museum of American History—Smithsonian Institution, Washington, D.C.; The Frederick Douglass Museum, D.C.; The Museum of Fine Arts, Boston; The Museum of African Art, New York; The Heritage Center Museum of Lancaster County, Pennsylvania; and The Eli Leon Collection.

C O N T E N T S

HIDDEN IN
PLAIN VIEW

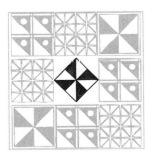

The Heritage of an Oral Tradition: The Transmission of Secrets in African American Culture

A Foreword
by Cuesta Benberry

IN THE YEARS SINCE THE CIVIL WAR ENDED, BITS AND PIECES OF orally transmitted information about secret codes, camouflaged symbols, and disguised signposts that were part of the Underground Railroad experience have emerged. Oft-repeated were oral accounts of escaping slaves, traveling on foot in unfamiliar territories, recognizing strangers' homes as places of sanctuary by means of prearranged signals. One story described the small wooden, painted black coachman figure, used as a hitching post or as a yard decoration, that also functioned as a signpost for fugitive slaves. When the black coachman's lantern was lighted, the escapees were alerted they had reached a safe haven. When the lantern was not lit, the slaves understood they should journey onward. Another story concerning quilts and secret encoded messages has engendered much controversy among historians. There were certain patterned patchwork quilts (often the Jacob's Ladder pattern, renamed the Underground Railroad pattern) hung outside the Underground Railroad supporters' homes that signaled the slaves had reached a safe haven. Some scholars denied the Jacob's Ladder design was even available for quiltmaking in antebellum America. They claimed the quilt design had not yet been invented, and so could not have contained secret messages recognizable to fugitives traveling on the Underground Railroad.

As all of the Underground Railroad signals-to-slaves stories were orally transmitted and lacked corroboration in written documentation, it was presumed the stories lacked credibility. In his book *Slave Testimony,* noted historian John Blassingame challenged the practice of scholars who rejected any truth of the black slaves' stories because they were oral testimonies. He stated, "Because of his traditional fascination with the written word, the American historian when confronted with oral lore . . . has no methodological tools applicable to them."

Oral testimonies were endemic to many of the enslaved blacks. In slave-holding states, it was actually illegal to teach slaves to read and write, and so most of those in bondage were bereft of the means of written communication. Moreover, the backgrounds of the slaves must be taken into consideration. As the prominent artist Bing Davis once remarked, "Slaves were not brought to America. Africans were brought to America, and there they were enslaved." The captured people, mainly from West and Central Africa, came from different environments, spoke different languages, and had different customs and mores. Yet for the majority of them, a shared and unifying element was the heritage of an oral tradition. In a number of different tribes, the most honored person was the griot, or storyteller, who committed to memory the entire history of the tribe, which he then taught to a younger member of the group. Thus each succeeding generation was assured the tribe's historical record was retained and could be recited orally. When the Africans were brought to America, their strong oral tradition accompanied them.

An astonishing example of the survival of the African oral tradition within the contemporary African American community is the Underground Railroad Quilt Code. Handed down orally, generation to generation since antebellum days, the Underground Railroad Quilt Code was recently revealed by recitation to Jacqueline L. Tobin and Raymond G. Dobard, Ph.D., by Ozella McDaniel Williams of Charleston, South Carolina. The Quilt Code is a mystery-laden, secret communication system of employing quiltmaking terminology as a message map for black slaves escaping on the Underground Railroad. Deciphering the code had both explicit and implicit ramifications for Jacqueline Tobin and Raymond Dobard. They learned what the words and phrases of the code meant to the fugitive slaves who used it over 150 years ago. By engaging in a vast amount of research, authors Tobin and Dobard have established a significant linkage between the Underground Railroad effort, escaping slaves, and the American patchwork quilt.

The Importance of the Decorative Arts in African American History

A Foreword
by Floyd Coleman, Ph.D.

IN *HIDDEN IN PLAIN VIEW: A SECRET STORY OF QUILTS AND THE Underground Railroad* Jacqueline Tobin and Raymond G. Dobard, Ph.D., tell a story of migration of a people and their culture. Migration, whether forced or voluntary, is a powerful fundamental dimension of the African American experience. Movement of people from West and Central Africa to the Caribbean and to the port cities of North America—Charleston, Savannah, New Orleans, Jamestown— begins the creation of a pan-African cultural heritage—shaped by chattel slavery and the struggle for freedom. Tobin and Dobard reveal that the enslaved Africans and their descendants were not hapless individuals, but ones who remembered or were taught their past, and through the materials available began to reconstruct themselves in the United States, a new very restricted environment. By firmly linking the art of quiltmaking to the struggle for freedom, the authors advance our understanding and appreciation of the role of women, of free blacks, and others who aided the cause of black liberation.

This study shows how quilts are part of the warp and weft of African American history and culture. The authors show how quilt patterns and stitches were used in the struggle for freedom—as codes that could be read by enslaved blacks as they traveled along the Underground Railroad. These authors have explored the techniques, the lore, and the iconography of African American quilts. Through sound scholarship and intimate knowledge of quilts and those who make them, the authors have provided another level of understanding of how the decorative arts—particularly quilts—go far beyond their functional nature. Tobin and Dobard have shown the beauty, the grace, the mastery, the spirituality, the sensuality, and the communicative power of quilts. They tell how these attributes are the threads of a quilting tradition that still lives in a myriad of ways in African American communities across the United States. The authors call our attention to the connections between the quilt as an instrument of freedom in the nineteenth century and as a didactic medium for the story quilts and the art quilts of today.

The energy, vitality, and meaning of the quilt resonates in the songs, the sermons, and the dances of African Americans. The authors have shown that a hegemonic dimension is attained through stitching pieces of cloth to create quilt tops of extraordinary beauty and meaning. The quilts discussed in this volume define and embody the manifestations of the African American experience, stitch by stitch, over time and space. Tobin and Dobard have taken quilt scholarship to another level. They have revealed that quilts are at once sources of pleasure, information, and meaning, and are central to understanding the history peoples of African ancestry in North America.

Secret African Signs Encoded in African American Quilts*

A Foreword

by Maude Southwell Wahlman, Ph.D.

Dorothy and Dale Thompson Professor of Global Arts, University of Missouri-Kansas City

WHEN AFRICAN RELIGIOUS IDEAS APPEARED IN THE NEW WORLD, they often assumed new forms and meanings and were transmitted in unprecedented ways. As essential tools for survival, these ideas were encoded in a multiplicity of forms, including architecture, dance, funerary practices, narratives, rituals, speech, music, and other visual arts, especially textiles. Arts preserve cultural traditions even when the social context of traditions changes, yet the codes are neither simple nor easy

---

* Sections of this essay are derived from a chapter entitled "Hidden Charms," from the forthcoming book *Souls Grown Deep: African American Vernacular Art of the South,* edited by Bill Arnett and Maude Southwell Wahlman, to be published by the Schomburg Center for African American Research, a branch of the New York Public Library.

to decipher. Sometimes forms endure while the meanings once associated
with them shift; in other instances, meanings persist and the shapes evolve.
Knowledge of ideas and techniques for creating arts are not necessarily
verbalized, written down, or expressly transmitted within a family, nor are
all levels of meaning always known to everyone in a community. Some
African Americans, and most Americans in general, are thoroughly un-
aware of these cultural traditions. One challenge is to examine which ideas
can be traced back to African cultures. A bigger challenge is to understand
the transmutations and creolizations that occur as each generation impro-
vises upon previous visual traditions and leads us ahead.

Africans who came to the New World brought with them many memories: memories of social organizations, religious values, and technological
skills. When combined with the memories of people from nearby areas
of Africa, or people from remote parts of Africa, a considerable body of
knowledge was preserved and perpetuated in America. But this knowledge
was often hidden, encoded in decorative arts, arts which were appreciated
and continued for their decorative qualities. Often the meanings originally
associated with the symbols were lost over time.

Scholars are just now beginning to unravel the numerous ways in
which valuable African skills, values, and ways of organizing ideas were
and are encoded in many art forms. We are learning to read symbolic elements that have been passed on from one generation to the next, not
through genetics, but through cultural memories. Quilts were one of
many media used to encode cultural knowledge. Three themes can be explored to explain continuities between African American quilting and
African cultural knowledge: technical skills, secret scripts, and charm-
making traditions. As Bill Arnett has written,

> Every great quilt, whether it be a patchwork, appliqué, or strip
> quilt, is a potential Rosetta stone. Quilts represent one of the

most highly evolved systems of writing in the New World. Every combination of colors, every juxtaposition or intersection of line and form, every pattern, traditional or idiosyncratic, contain data that can be imparted in some form or another to anyone. All across Africa, geometric designs, the syntax of quilt tops, have been used to encode symbolic or secret knowledge. Bodily decoration and costumes, architectural ornamentation (including painting), and relief carving have been primary media. Geometric designs painted on homes were reportedly formerly used as a means of covert social protest against apartheid by Sotho-Tswana women in South Africa.

Souls Grown Deep,
Arnett and Wahlman

In the ways in which quilts are constructed, we find information about how West African textiles were constructed, mainly from narrow strips, about the width of the human hand. In the ways in which designs were borrowed, improvised upon, and jazzed up, we find clues to secret African symbol systems, which we also see in African American vernacular painting.

African secret society signs and symbols are still hidden in decorative textile designs. Examples include Bogolanfini cloth painted by Bamana women in Mali; Adinkra cloth stamped by Ashanti men in Ghana; Adire cloth painted by Yoruba women with designs said to have been given to them by Oshun, the goddess of wealth and fertility in Nigeria; Epke (Leopard) society cloth resist-dyed by Ejagham women with *nsibidi* secret society signs in Nigeria; and Kuba cloth woven with designs which allude to the central African Kongo cosmogram, a diamond or a cross which represents the four moments of the sun or the soul: birth, life, death, and rebirth in the watery ancestral realm. Scripts are also considered protective and thus bits of writing, Christian, Islamic, or indigenous secret signs, are enclosed in West African charms.

This tradition of encoding secret signs in textile designs, mostly done by women, continued in the New World, where remembered African signs were combined to create unique new creolized symbol systems. Examples include a Brazilian cloth embroidered with designs, called *Points*, for a Yoruba god, Ogun, and Suriname capes embroidered by women with designs derived from a Maroon script called *Afaka*, which is based on Adinkra symbols from Ghana and *nsibidi* signs from Nigeria. Cuban *Abakua* society costumes are based on Nigerian ones, with light and dark squares to represent leopard spots and valued religious principles. Haitian Vodou flags are decorated with sequins arranged in *Veve* signs which refer to various remembered Yoruba and Fon gods.

Throughout the United States South, as insulation against the cold, people have decorated the interior walls of their homes with cutouts from books, newspapers, and magazines. Some African American quilts look like those walls, because for many, there was an additional religious meaning associated with those multiple images. Unhappy, neglected ancestral spirits could be thwarted from their mischievous ways because they would be distracted by and need to read and decipher all this chopped-up and discontinuous text before they could do any harm. In much the same way that quilts provided physical warmth and spiritual safety, the wall collages linked African Americans' most corporeal needs with their most metaphysical ones, and can be traced to the African belief that writing is considered protective and is thus enclosed in charms. The form has changed but the protective idea persists. Romare Bearden drew upon this African American tradition of collaging walls with protective images in his famous collaged art. Quilters drew on this collage tradition in their improvised quilts which feature multiple patterns, and thus function as protective bedcovers in several ways.

In the United States, various African and African Latin American and Caribbean signs appear in historic and contemporary African American quilts (*Signs and Symbols: African Images in African-American Quilts*, Wahlman, pp. 75–101). My recent research concentrates on the convergence of secret African symbols and Masonic signs, which were used to run the Underground Railroad. Women sewed Masonic aprons and other Masonic textiles and knew of the multiple levels of meaning attached to symbols. The nineteenth-century quilter and Eastern Star society leader Harriet Powers used these symbols in her quilts and we see references to her control of Fon symbols from the Republic of Benin in West Africa, Kongo symbols from Central Africa, Christian symbols, and Masonic signs in her textiles, including her own Masonic apron. It features an embroidered cross, the cosmogram of the Kongo people, an appliquéd light sun for life, as well as a dark "midnight" sun for the undersea world of the ancestors.

Jacki Tobin and I have been trading information on Masonic aspects of American history, and *Hidden in Plain View* validates the tradition of women encoding secret signs in their textile designs. We find more and more documentation for cooperation between members of African American and Anglo-American Masonic societies, as many abolitionists were Masons. Many African American families have knowledge of how artifacts were encoded with secret signs used to communicate vital information on how to proceed on the Underground Railroad to freedom. My hope is that these families who have so freely shared their knowledge of quilting styles, techniques, and symbols will also share their family stories about the Underground Railroad and how information was encoded and passed on.

In the ways in which symbolic designs were included in decorative pieced patterns and appliquéd designs, we also find evidence of remembered charm-making traditions which persist also in African American vernacular sculpture. The African American charm, called a Mojo or a "Hand," is often a small square made of red flannel which is carried in the pocket or worn around the neck. Zora Neale Hurston recorded numerous instructions for how to make these charms. One also sees them on African American quilts, particularly those using the Nine Patch pattern. Sara Mary Taylor even made a quilt with both a blue hand and a red square, indicating her mastery of the symbols. The "Vodou doll" seen on African American quilts can be traced back to the cloth "Pacquet Kongo" charm brought to Haiti by the Kongo people of Central Africa, where it was referred to as an *nkisi,* or "the medicines of God."

Contemporary African American fine artists have just begun to rediscover folk art traditions and to incorporate family oral histories into their arts. Both fine and folk, or vernacular, African American arts are sophisticated in terms of levels of meaning that one can learn to read. My research, which began many years ago with African arts, concentrates on those hidden African symbols which resurface in the New World, in all African American arts.

Jacki Tobin is to be applauded for being in the right place at the right time, and having enough faith to go back again and again to listen to the story of one family's efforts to encode knowledge in their quilt tops. And one salutes her partnership with Raymond Dobard, whose knowledge of quilting technology is so outstanding. Their persistence has saved and revealed one aspect of this encoding process which is vital to our understanding of African American culture and its myriad contributions to American life. If others can be as attentive, and persistent, we will find many more examples. If young people will interview their grandparents before this knowledge is lost, it will benefit all of us.

As William Ferris is fond of saying, "in Africa when an older person dies, a library burns." That can also be said for elders in African American society. The WPA narratives saved some knowledge, but the questions asked were often naïve.

"Write This Down"

by Jacqueline Tobin

IN 1994 I TRAVELED TO CHARLESTON, SOUTH CAROLINA, TO LEARN more about the sweet-grass baskets unique to this area and to hear the stories of the African American craftswomen who make them. Charleston is rich in history. A port city, where the Ashley River meets the Cooper to form (as locals like to say) the beginnings of the Atlantic Ocean, Charleston today is a place whose buildings and culture reflect the combined and separate histories of American and African American peoples. It is unique as the location where black slaves first set foot on American soil and once outnumbered the white population four to one.

A walk through the historic district of Charleston is like a walk through the corridors of American Southern history. Here, one is confronted by all the hustle and bustle of the retentions and re-creations of a bygone era. At the heart of historic Charleston is an imposing brick enclosure with open sides, known as the Old Marketplace. It looks very much as it did over one hundred years ago, as it still defines the length of the district. As it was in years gone by, the Marketplace is still the center of commerce for the area. Under the roof of the structure, long wooden tables, laid end-to-end, go on for blocks to create two narrow avenues for selling wares. As early as 1841 it was a marketplace for fresh vegetables, fish, meats, and other goods brought to Charleston from the surrounding farms and plantations and other coastal ports and faraway lands; it is still a vendor's market, but with stark contrasts between the old and the new. African American women sit by pails of sweet grass and weave baskets much as their African ancestors did over a hundred years ago. But these craftswomen, many of them descendants of slaves, are now surrounded by merchants of flea market trinkets, Southern memorabilia, and newer, cheaper baskets from China and Thailand.

The smell of the daily ocean catch or freshly slaughtered meats is no longer the predominant early morning smell of the Marketplace. Today the aroma of freshly baked cookies and newly ground coffee beans from the gourmet shops surrounding the area compete for attention. Certain sounds can still be heard; the din of tourists and locals alike crowding the streets and trying to avoid the horses, their hooves providing the percussive rhythm for this city as they clop loudly over original cobblestone streets. Carriages are drawn around the district, past the Custom House and on toward the Battery, where decorative wrought-iron fences accentuate the largess of old historic homes. Taverns and brothels have given way to fern bars and upscale hotels touting Southern hospitality and cuisine. Newly restored, on a lesser traveled street, is the original slave mart, now a historical museum, whose presence jars us into remembering a less civil piece of the history of this Southern port city.

As I walked the aisles of the Marketplace, I found myself standing in front of a stall lined with quilts of all sizes, colors, and patterns. I was drawn in by these piles of quilts, as long-forgotten memories of my grand-mother's quilt box, filled with her handmade quilts, were brought to mind. Before I could do much looking or reminiscing, an elderly African American woman, dressed in brightly colored, geometrically patterned African garb, slowly walked up to me from the back of the stall. She motioned me to follow her to the back, where an old metal folding chair sat surrounded by more quilts. "Look," she said. She chose one of the quilts from the pile, unrolled it, and while pointing to it said, "Did you know that quilts were used by slaves to communicate on the Underground Railroad?" The old quilter continued to speak but I could not hear her clearly in the midst of the noise of the Marketplace around us. I wasn't sure why she was telling me, a complete stranger, this unusual story. I listened politely for a short while. When I didn't ask any questions, she stopped talking. I purchased a beautiful, hand-tied quilt and left with her flyer advertising "historic Charleston Marketplace" quilts.

I returned home with my quilt and memories of Charleston. I hung my quilt and laid my memories aside. I didn't think too much about my conversation with this quilter until several months later when I came across her flyer again. I remembered the story she had started to tell me and I wondered about it. I had never heard such a story or read about it in any books. Was there more to the story? The flyer listed the quilter's name and phone number. I decided to call Mrs. Ozella McDaniel Williams and see if she would be willing to tell me more. When she answered the phone, I reminded her of who I was and asked if I might hear more about how quilts were used on the Underground Railroad. She told me curtly to call back the next evening, which I did. At that time she said, "I can't speak to you about this right now." When I tried pressing her, she laughed quietly and whispered into the phone, "Don't worry, you'll get the story when you are ready." And then she hung up.

Ozella had now added an element of intrigue to the already fascinating story. I was hooked. What did she mean by "you'll get the story when you're ready"? I felt I had to explore the story further. If she wouldn't talk, perhaps others would. I began to contact every African American quilter and quilt scholar I could find. I traveled down the Mississippi from St. Louis to New Orleans, stopping to visit quilters and scholars. I toured plantations and slave quarters, looking for clues. Before long, I was speaking to a fairly close-knit circle of people that included art historians, African American quilters, African textile experts, and folklorists. Most of them had heard that quilts had been used as a means of secret communication on the Underground Railroad, but none were exactly sure how. Some referenced particular quilt patterns, some mentioned the stitching, and others cited specific colors. I was not able to find any slave quilts that could verify these stories. Most quilt scholars agreed that few slave quilts had survived the constant strain of excessive use, the poor quality of fabric they had probably been sewn from, and the continual washing in harsh lye soap that would eventually cause them to disintegrate.

As a white person conducting research into African American scholarship, I was hesitant at times to continue. Some people were reluctant to share family stories with me. At one point I suggested that Dr. Raymond Dobard, one of the scholars I was conversing with, continue my research by contacting Ozella himself. I was hoping that she would speak more freely to another African American. Raymond, an art history professor at Howard University, a renowned quilter, and a known expert on African American quilts as they relate to the Underground Railroad, seemed to me to be the perfect person to pursue this research with Ozella. However, when I made my suggestion, Raymond insisted that I was the one with whom Ozella felt comfortable telling the story initially and thus should be the one to pursue it. He told me to be patient and that I would indeed get the story when I was ready. With his encouragement I continued my research.

Three years after first hearing the story, I had come full circle with my research, but there were still missing pieces. I could add nothing new to the information that was already out there. Still lacking was an elaboration of the story connecting quilts and the Underground Railroad. I was hoping for a final link connecting all the quilt stories with details. My intuition told me that Ozella knew more than what she'd already told me. The only way to find out would be to return to Charleston and see if she would speak to me again.

Without contacting her first, I arranged a return visit to Charleston. If Ozella was reluctant to speak, I didn't want to give her any time to think about it and turn me down without my ability to plead my case in person. Besides, I had done my homework, and maybe, I thought, I was now "ready" to receive the story in full. Armed with information and questions, I felt the time was right.

Upon my arrival, I took a carriage tour around the historic Charleston district. I wanted to immerse myself once again in the flavor of the Old South before attempting to talk with Ozella. As the carriage passed the Marketplace, I turned to look, my eyes straining to recognize my quilter friend's face. I recognized her immediately, sitting in the same location, amidst her tables of quilts, just as I had seen her three years prior. Today she was dressed all in white. She had on white slacks and a white blouse decorated with a huge lavender flower hand-painted on the front. She wore a large straw hat with a white band that had the same lavender flower painted on it as well.

I completed my carriage ride and walked slowly down the aisles of the Marketplace. I was nervous about meeting her again. Would she remember me? I wondered. What if I had come this far and she still wouldn't speak to me? Or, worse yet, what if she really didn't know anything more than she had already told me? With notebook in hand I took a deep breath and hesitantly approached her. Her back was turned to me as she stood quietly arranging her quilts. I cleared my throat to get her attention. When she turned, I tried to hand her my business card and started to explain who I was and why I was there. With a wave of her hand, brushing my card away, she interrupted me and said, "I don't care who you is. You is people and that is all that matters. Bring over some of those quilts and make a seat for yourself beside me. Get yourself comfortable."

I hesitated, but only briefly. If she was ready to talk, I was ready to listen. I was concerned about sitting on her handmade works of art, but she didn't seem to care. She positioned herself on the metal folding chair, moving quilts to either side of her and around her. I chose several rolled quilts and brought them over in front of her. After placing them on the ground, I sat down in front of her. From this position I was looking directly up into Ozella's face. She pulled her folding chair even closer to me. I became aware that she was now physically creating a space around us, obviously meant only for her and me. After seating herself on the folding chair she leaned down toward me, one hand resting on her knee, her index finger pointing to my notepad. She pushed her straw hat farther back on her head and with her other hand she directed me, "Write this down."

From the moment she said those words until she finished speaking about three hours later, time stood still. The normal chaos of Saturday morning at the Marketplace ceased to exist for us. Nothing and no one entered this space to disturb us. It was as if what she was going to say was for my ears only and that this time and space had been set aside for me to hear it. I felt that fate was honoring this moment. With a faraway look in her eyes, reciting something from memory, Ozella instructed me on what to write, stopping now and then only to ask me to read it back to her.

It took all my journalistic energies to focus on writing the words she spoke and to not get lost in the art of her telling. I was the student; she was the teacher. I was the transcriber; she the storyteller. At that moment, I knew that I was one of only a trusted few people who, down through history, had been told to listen carefully and remember the words she was speaking. Sitting beside this elderly black woman, surrounded by a sea of

her handiwork, I felt that she was inviting me to share in her family stories and memories and become a part of an oral tradition that had allowed
her culture to survive. I was no longer the journalist in search of a story.
My role was to be much different. I felt that Ozella had very purposefully
created an atmosphere where I was to receive this information.
Surrounding us were only the sounds of her ancestors, family members
like her mother and grandmother before her, passing words of information from one woman to another for safekeeping. During this time, I was
aware of nothing but her voice and her message and the awesome responsibility she was giving me to write the story down. Seated at the feet of an
older woman, I was conscious that we were taking part in a time-honored
women's ritual of passing on wisdom from one generation to another. I
was aware that we were bridging not only a gap of generations but also
one of race. We were transcending age, stereotypes, and boundaries.

Until now, the story Ozella revealed to me has never been written down
and shared with the public. It has been passed down orally in her family for
generations; Ozella received it from her mother, who received it from
Ozella's grandmother. The story has survived in the memories of those
women and men who have committed themselves to remembering it. I felt
that Ozella was commanding me to break the silence. I am indebted to her
for trusting me with her story, and I have honored it without embellishment.

Raymond was the obvious choice to coauthor this book. As a scholar on
quilts and the Underground Railroad as well as a well-known African
American quilter, Raymond recognized that, as Ozella had originally told
me, quilt patterns and stitching provided an ingenious method of
Underground Railroad communication. With the admonition and blessings
of Mrs. Ozella McDaniel Williams, we are passing this story on; a true tale
of survival, skill, transcendence, and memory. The following are the words
recited to me by Ozella in Charleston, South Carolina, on May 11, 1996.
Raymond and I have named this the Underground Railroad Quilt Code.

OZELLA'S
UNDERGROUND RAILROAD
QUILT CODE

There are *five square knots* on the quilt every *two inches apart*. They escaped on the *fifth knot* on the *tenth pattern* and went to Ontario, Canada.

The **monkey wrench** turns the **wagon wheel**

toward Canada on a **bear's paw** trail

to the **crossroads**. Once they got to the **crossroads** they

dug a **log cabin** on the ground.

Shoofly told them to dress up in

cotton and satin **bow ties** and go to the cathedral

church, get married and exchange double wedding rings. **Flying geese**

 stay on the **drunkard's path**

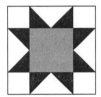

and follow the **stars**.

At first reading, one is struck by the imagery and poetic descriptions. But beneath the language lies a much deeper, much larger story, a story that reaches back to Africa and forward to the Carolinas, connecting African symbols to familiar quilt patterns, all tied together with the sounds of spirituals and the African American struggle to escape the bonds of slavery.

Stitching Ideas into Patterns:

Methodology in the Writing of
HIDDEN IN PLAIN VIEW

by Raymond G. Dobard, Ph.D.

WHEN JACQUELINE TOBIN FIRST CONTACTED ME AND TOLD ME about Ozella McDaniel Williams's story, I was awestruck. Jacki's words were as bright as the sunlight streaming into my apartment on a Sunday morning in May of 1996. She spoke almost in a whisper on the phone as if she were a continent away. She recited the "story" and cautiously asked if I had heard anything like it before. I assured her that I hadn't, and that in my opinion she had found what I and other quilt history researchers had been seeking for years. She'd found an Underground Railroad Code. The quilt pattern names combined with traveling instructions made sense to me. As an art historian, my years of studying iconography (the meaning of images) of various cultures ranging from the art of early Christianity, to subject matter in the art of both the German artist Käthe Kollwitz and the African American painter Romare Bearden, to my research into African American quilts and the Underground Railroad enabled me to recognize that what Jacki was reciting was some form of code. Excited as I was by the prospect of conducting research on this new find, as an art historian and quilt history investigator, I knew how difficult it would be to substantiate the code as one used on the Underground Railroad. When Jacki asked me to join her in writing about Ozella's Underground Railroad Quilt Code, I realized the challenge that we faced.

Since the field of African American quilt history is relatively new, Jacki and I acknowledge that ideas and theories might not always be conclusively proven as much as presented for serious consideration. Our methodology and interpretation will open the field to further exploration and to the piecing together of ideas and the making of connections. Because the Quilt Code was recited in story form, we began our research by considering the relevance of storytelling in the African American community, and by examining well-known stories about quilts and the Underground Railroad to determine what clues they might contain. We observed that quilt patterns were often essential components of the stories, just as they are in Ozella's story code. We saw quilt patterns as visual keys with the potential to open the code. As we delved further, we confirmed our knowledge that quilt patterns had their own individual stories to tell. Together, the stories and the patterns made it possible for us to interpret the meaning of Ozella's Underground Railroad Quilt Code. In this book we place stories and patterns side by side so that they might illuminate each other to the benefit of our understanding the code.

We memorized Ozella's story and looked to related sources for evidence connecting quilts to the Underground Railroad. We found a whole host of clues, tools we used to position the Quilt Code within its cultural and historical context: slavery in nineteenth-century America. Since many who were enslaved came from Africa and brought their culture with them, we needed to know and to appreciate African culture as it existed in Africa, and how it continued in adapted form on American soil.

We submersed ourselves in African history to broaden our knowledge and to acquire a deeper understanding of its rich culture. We respected the oral tradition, the essence of African and African American history. We investigated African cultural antecedents and American quiltmaking precedents seeking links to the Underground Railroad Quilt story-code. We sought a visual language, one predicated upon geometric designs and distinctive stitches. We examined both African and American textile traditions, keeping in mind that the Quilt Code is an African American composition in which geometric quilt patterns are prominent. Stitches were also of interest to us because Ozella disclosed the use of stitches by slaves in forming a language to "talk" about paths to freedom. We had to ask ourselves how African and American elements were combined in signs, symbols, stitches, memory triggers we call mnemonic devices, and quiltmaking. Why were quilts the chosen medium to conceal and yet reveal a means of escape? How would an enslaved people who had little knowledge, if any, of the land beyond the plantation be able to chart a path out of bondage? Questions were coming faster than answers. But we suspected that clues existed in the use of patterns mentioned in the code.

Thanks to many publications of quilt patterns and their meanings, including the early work of Marie D. Webster (1915), Ruth E. Finley (1929), the joint publication of Carrie A. Hall and Rose G. Kretsinger (1935, 1947), and the contemporary encyclopedias covering geometric as well as appliqué patterns compiled by Barbara Brackman (1979, 1984, 1993), we were able to trace American quilt patterns and see how they were used. For quilt stories and for the contemporary interpretation of the patterns and their links to African American history, we turned to many scholarly works, including the publications of Pat Ferrero, Elaine Hedges, Julie Silber, Sandi Fox, Cuesta Benberry, Gladys-Marie Fry, John Michael Vlach, and Maude S. Wahlman.

Patchwork quilts were readable objects in nineteenth-century America. Quilt patterns, in particular the geometric ones, were named according to geographic regions and to prevailing social concerns. Two examples are Bear's Paw and Job's Tears. The pattern we call Bear's Paw was known as such in mid-nineteenth-century western Pennsylvania and Ohio. The very same pattern was called Duck's Foot-in-the-Mud on Long Island, New York. And for Philadelphia Quakers the pattern was named Hand of Friendship. The design known in 1800 as Job's Tears became Slave Chain by 1825 and Texas Tears by 1840 because of social opposition to slavery and interest in the Texas territory. After the Civil War, the pattern was called Rocky Road to Kansas or Kansas Troubles. The last name the pattern received was Endless Chain (Hall and Kretsinger, p. 64). This early nineteenth-century pattern bears a striking resemblance to the early twentieth-century Double Wedding Ring pattern. We suspect the Job's Tears pattern to be the pattern referred to as Double Wedding Ring in Ozella's Underground Railroad Quilt Code. Some quilts served as billboards or banners for women to express their social or moral convictions through the names and meanings they gave the patterns. Patterned textiles also conveyed meaning in nineteenth-century Africa as, for example, the Ukara cloth of Cross River, Nigeria, wherein geometric designs pertained to the Leopard Secret Guardian Society. In both American quilt patterns and the Ukara cloth, the geometric designs conveyed messages and told stories. Our research also revealed a similarity in the composition of particular geometric patterns in American quilts and African textiles. Were there any real connections here? And how did these patterns function?

Some geometric motifs surfaced in conjunction with secret societies throughout West Africa. When we took a closer look at these secret societies, their use of geometric designs, and their authority over the social, moral, and religious life of the community, we learned about the Poro Society for men and the Sande for women, which, like other secret societies, were part of the pattern of life and the structured culture in Africa. They often utilized geometrically configured signs and symbols. Stories were also incorporated in the societies' teaching of morals and history. Was there an African American equivalent? We wondered.

Within a short period of time we found out. When reading about the narrative appliqué Bible quilts of the famed nineteenth-century African American quilter Harriet Powers, we were struck by her rendering of Jacob's Ladder and intrigued by references to Masonic symbols (see color photo section). Like most scholars in the field of African American quilt research, we wondered if Powers was a member of an Eastern Star women's association. When researching the images in her quilts and their possible Masonic meanings, we learned about the Prince Hall Masons, an African American fraternal organization founded by Prince Hall in the late eighteenth century. Not only were the Prince Hall Masons comparable to the African secret societies in terms of their community roles, but they also used geometric motifs as signs and symbols. Might there be a connection between the Prince Hall Masons, the Underground Railroad, Ozella's story code, and what appears to be shared interest in a geometric language? And what of the stories told about the Prince Hall Masons? There we were again, in the middle of a dialogue between patterns and stories. We probed the correlation in meaning and use of geometric symbols and we listened to the Masonic stories. Having considered the stories and the patterns side by side, we then focused primarily on the stories and the relevance that storytelling had to a people of African descent.

Supportive of our theories are recent interpretive exhibitions of African art, such as the 1996 New York show entitled *Memory: Luba Art and the Making of History,* with a catalog written by curators Mary Nooter

Roberts and Allen F. Roberts. This seminal show and inspiring catalog, which presented a scholarly reconsideration of decoration and meaning in African art, demonstrated how African art objects were encoded with "decorative" designs that were really mnemonic devices which only the trained eye could read. This sounded familiar to us. Might not patterns on a quilt top have a similar function?

Thanks to the Luba exhibition, we learned about the *lukasa,* the small rectangular wooden boards are pieces of sculpture on which patterns are engraved and beads are tacked down to form what appear to be random groupings. In actuality the groupings, as well as the colors of the beads, serve to trigger memory for those trained to recognize the arrangements. One example that Mary Nooter Roberts cites is a *lukasa* whereon one isolated blue bead represents a king, chief, or title holder. If that same blue bead is encircled by a number of smaller white beads, the arrangement stands for a king, chief, or title holder located within a determined space, a compound. A row of small white beads positioned to form a diagonal line indicates a road, a pathway, or a route. This same motif might also represent migration. A row of stitching knots left visible on a quilt top could easily simulate this *lukasa* bead arrangement. Are knots on a quilt top a translation of the *lukasa* visual language? The many motifs formed by bead arrangements work in tandem with engraved patterns and sculptural forms to create a complex visual language. As with any language, a word or a motif is understood in context. The meaning of a particular motif may change given the context (see Nooter Roberts-Roberts, *Memory,* pp. 117–47). *Lukasa,* therefore, translates as "memory boards." In 1993 Mary Nooter was curator of an earlier exhibition, *Secrecy: African Art That Conceals and Reveals,* and editor of the publication by the same title. Art, knowledge, and secrecy in Africa were the focus of that important work, which demonstrated how history, religious beliefs, and cultural stories were translated into designs and exhibited for all to see but few to read. We realized that it was possible to hide messages in plain view using patterned, "decorative" designs. We asked ourselves the obvious question: Did these African traditions, celebrated in what is today Senegambia, Angola, the Republic of the Kongo, and other regions from where many slaves were brought to the Charleston area, have any influence on encoding quilts? Did the American quiltmaking tradition, in which geometric patterns were given names and meaning, invite appropriation by black slaves and their descendants seeking ways and means to continue their own encoding traditions? Is Ozella's story-code a cultural hybrid, mixing African encoding traditions with American quilt patterning conventions? Can we consider the African American quilt a form of *lukasa*? Was the *lukasa* limited to the sculptural boards, or might there be other forms of *lukasa*? How were colors used in this tradition? In Africa there was one person who might answer our questions: the *griot*.

Stories were the primary medium of the African *griot*, whose task it was to memorize all important historical events for the village community and to recite history in a creative fashion. The African griot was the living repository of history in Africa and on foreign soil in the Americas. Anthropologists, historians, and folklorists have studied the continuation of this African tradition in plantation life and beyond emancipation. In fact, the Gullah people of the Sea Islands off the coast of South Carolina and Georgia have long been the focus of study for many scholars, such as Margaret Washington Creel, who wrote *A Peculiar People: Slave Religion and Community-Culture Among the Gullahs*.

The telling of history continues today within the African American community as stories are surfacing at family reunions where elders are breaking with decades of silence and are telling their stories, no longer in fear of retribution from vindictive whites or of being ridiculed by loved ones of younger, disbelieving generations. Many African American elders are saying, "Now it can be told." We must listen and respect their stories if we, both black and white, are to preserve a valuable part of our American heritage. This is why we, the authors of *Hidden in Plain View*, looked first to related stories about quilts, maps, and the Underground Railroad in order to glean information that might assist us in understanding Ozella's Underground Railroad quilt story.

We are acutely aware that stories are woven through the fabric of the African American community, binding individuals to their ancestors and to each other. These stories are the remnants of a history that is still being written. To follow the stories is to trace African American history: from Africa to America, from bondage to freedom, from survival to triumph, and the creation of an African American culture.

Stories about the Underground Railroad have circulated in the African American community for generations. Several of these stories have made their way into print in the form of children's books. Some stories have formed the basis for more extensive scholarship in folklore studies, African American quilting, and spirituals. Of the many stories told about the Underground Railroad, one is recurrent. It has been found in three different parts of the country, told by three different people, at three different times, and in three intriguingly similar yet unique ways. In each the story line is essentially the same: quilts were used as maps on the Underground Railroad. In each, particular quilt patterns are identified. Is it coincidence that the patterns and the story line are the same or is it an example of how oral tradition keeps history alive?

When we reached this point in structuring a methodology, we felt as though we had climbed Jacob's Ladder. We had encountered much on the way up, from the many stories and patterns we investigated. Our vantage point was now from the upper rung of an intellectual ladder, from which we were able to see many facets of the African American quilt and the path described in the Quilt Code. The code that carried us back to Africa, returned us to America, and finally transported us to Canada was now in plain sight.

Based on my knowledge as a quilter/historian, Jacki's expertise in women's stories, and our combined research, we were able to formulate a theory of how this Quilt Code may have worked for slaves escaping on the Underground Railroad. Our interpretation of the code is based in part upon informed conjecture. While we believe that our research and the piecing together of our findings present a strong viable case, we do not claim that our "deciphering" of the code is infallible. Nor do we insist that our perspective is the only one for viewing the code. We have written the book in a way that encourages questions. We leave room for the reader to add her/his own ideas and thereby contribute to the growing body of knowledge. In the spirit of quiltmaking, we invite you to join us in juxtaposing ideas so that patterns and meanings are revealed.

Ideally we would have several of the special slave-made quilts containing the patterns and the stitching mentioned in Ozella's story-code to analyze. Unfortunately, the fragile nature of textiles, the hard use to which these quilts were exposed, the lye soap washing, the possible taking along of quilt-maps on the arduous journey north, and the lapse of over a century have mitigated against the survival of many slave-made quilts. Compounding this dearth of extant quilts was the popular misconception that precise geometrically patterned quilts were not made by blacks and were therefore dismissed during the cataloging of African American quilts. We have thus found ourselves obliged to reverse conventional procedures, having to present a theory before finding a wealth of tangible evidence. We do believe that with the publication of this book, however, many "hidden" African American quilts and perhaps even other Underground Railroad quilt codes will surface.

The African slave, despite the horrors of the Middle Passage,
did not sail to the New World alone. These African slaves
brought with them their metaphysical systems, their languages,
their terms for order and their expressive cultural practices
which even the horrendous Middle Passage and
the brutality of everyday life on the plantation
could not effectively obliterate.

HENRY LOUIS GATES,
AS QUOTED IN *TALK THAT TALK*
by Linda Goss and Marian Barnes

The Fabric of Heritage:
Africa and African American Quiltmaking

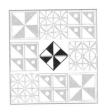

THE AFRICAN AMERICAN QUILT IS A CULTURAL HYBRID THAT ENJOYS encoding meaning through geometric patterns, abstract improvised designs, strip-piecing, bold, singing colors, and distinctive stitches. When we analyze these five elements of encoding meaning, we will see the African American quilt for what it is: a "fabric griot."

As a fabric griot the African American quilt is a communicator, conveying heritage as it once displayed a means for slaves to flee the plantation and journey to freedom. Although the African American quilt appears to be an everyday bedcover, it is more.

Communicating secrets using ordinary objects is very much a part of African culture, in which familiarity provides the perfect cover. Messages can be skillfully passed on through objects that are seen so often they become invisible. These objects are creative expressions of

African artisans and give tangible form to the cultural and religious ideas of their kingdoms.

Of the artists, the blacksmiths, those enigmatic men who possess power that is revered yet feared, and whose social position in sub-Saharan Africa is paradoxical, were sometimes shunned and yet enjoyed privileged positions, especially in Mande society, as revered creators, keepers of the fire, and form-givers of iron. They were believed to be favored by the gods and imbued with special power and knowledge. For the Mende of Sierra Leone, the blacksmiths were also the keepers of culture who imparted secret social and religious knowledge to young male initiates of the Poro Society. As leaders of secret societies, such as the Poro found throughout West Africa, the blacksmiths forged cultural norms into heritage.

In his book *The Mande Blacksmiths: Knowledge, Power, and Art in West Africa,* Patrick R. McNaughton explains that the blacksmith would literally keep the rhythm of the community through the use of his bellows. McNaughton, after observing the Mande blacksmiths at work and their surrounding community members in relation to them, refers to the blacksmiths' "patterns of rhythm that resemble drum beats, except that the percussive thrust of drumming is replaced by fluid gusts of air." He states further that the competency level of a young blacksmith would determine whether or not he developed a "sharp, crisp precision in his rhythms." Often, the rhythms became astonishingly complex. Each blacksmith, asserts McNaughton, would have his own favorite rhythms. Even the women grinding millet nearby would join the blacksmiths in creating an orchestrated performance of sound (McNaughton, pp. 24–25).*

The blacksmiths were not alone in preserving heritage. The griots, often storytelling musicians, were also the guardians of history. In a soci-

---

* See Bibliography for information on works cited throughout.

ety where a written language was not universal, their job was to mentally record and transmit ancestral lineage, customs, beliefs, events, names, dates, and legends from generation to generation. The griots learned and taught via an oral tradition, based on memory, aided by the use of specially designed mnemonic devices. Encoded staffs, stools, memory boards, sculpture, and textiles chronicled the history of a people. But only the griots and the diviners were able to read them.

"Talking drums" resounded throughout the forest and grasslands, carrying messages from kingdom to kingdom. The repeated tonal patterns created a language based on a rhythm and beat that can still be heard today in Africa as well as in American jazz.

Of the many types and peculiar sounds, the small two-headed hourglass drum played by the Yoruba of Dahomey and Nigeria is unique in that it is capable of reproducing all tones of speech. This particular drum, called *tama* by the Wolof, is known as *kalengu* to the Hausa. According to African musical specialist Francis Bebey, author of *African Music: A People's Art,* the hourglass drum transmits actual spoken messages due to the drum's design and the skill of the musician who plays "spoken phrases." In the case of tonal languages such as Yoruba or certain Bantu languages, the hourglass drum and tonal phrases are appropriate, Bebey contends (Bebey, p. 96).

The other type of "talking drum" that is well known is the slit drum, which varies in length from one to seven feet, with the average being three feet. This drum is carefully created by hollowing out the center of a tree trunk. A longitudinal slit with two tongues (one considered male, the other female) is carved into the resulting hollowed cylinder. Because the slit drum is capable of producing only two distinct notes, Bebey tells us that "for this reason, the messages are nearly always coded and consist of a series of metaphorical phrases that may be applied to various events of a similar nature" (Bebey, p. 96). He goes on to explain that some of the slit drums are given specific names drawn from proverbs, symbols, or riddles. Such as "Pain doesn't kill," "Death has no master," and "Birds don't steal from empty fields."

Drums are not interchangeable. Such is the case with the drum that tells of death and the drum used for dances. The "talking drums," then, speak about many things including impending danger (Bebey, p. 96). Given this wealth of percussive expression, is it any wonder that enslaved Africans and their descendants would be able to communicate even when forbidden to read or write?

Nearly all Africans brought to America as slaves came from West African societies where community cohesion was firmly ingrained and supported through a network of secret societies. Within this structure, men and women were taught the religious, social, sexual, and ethical mores of their communities. Social cohesion was enforced, and order throughout the society was established. Knowledge was passed on and cultural integrity maintained. Separate secret societies existed for men and women. There were severe consequences should the secrecy be broken. While many secret societies dotted the landscape of West Africa, two of the largest were the Poro for men and the Sande for women. These societies were almost universal features in coastal West Africa. Participation was mandatory for all men and women who lived in the areas where the Poro and Sande existed.

A description of the Poro and Sande secret societies sets the stage for a clearer understanding of some of the antecedents of African American culture. Secret societies, or "bush schools" as they were known because of their location, served as training centers for boys becoming men and girls becoming women. Each society was strictly divided by gender and membership determined largely through reaching the age of puberty.

The Poro secret society is for men only. It is a bush school in that its location is usually set out in the bush, hidden some distance away from the village compound. Initiates are subject to trials, including learning a new esoteric language. According to the anthropologist F. W. Butt-Thompson, the new language held secrets known only to Poro members, and was intended to help them sever all ties with their former lives as boys. In some cases, esoteric speech took the form of "passwords" (Butt-Thompson, p. 150).

For most Poro societies, as exemplified best in the Mande culture, it is the blacksmith who is the great one and whose job is sacred. It was the blacksmith, with his knowledge of herbs and medicine and his status in the community as revered elder, who performed the transforming rite of circumcision. As the blacksmith bends, molds, and transforms the iron he works with, he also symbolically transforms young boys into men.

Knowledge was imparted to them depending upon their attainment of different levels. Only members of the highest level would have received all the knowledge to be imparted. Out of the ten levels of the Poro secret society, only two have been revealed to outsiders. The tenth degree is described by Butt-Thompson:

> Finally, when he has passed through all the grades, which few do, when he has finally sworn the greatest oath of all, when he knows all the society's heart's secrets and that can be summed up in the sentence: I am through my knowledge of law and order and justice and morality, then, and not until then, he is an Elder, a man revered, honored, and obeyed. (p. 35)

The name "Poro" is itself an oath taken by the members when they say, "By Poro I swear [this is] unbreakable." The Poro society buildings are called lodges; the first known one dates back to the late seventeenth century. Butt-Thompson wrote:

Any freeman after a certain age may become a member of this association. On his admission he undergoes various ceremonies,
and is enjoined the strictest secrecy respecting them, which they
persevere as inviolable as the freemasons in Europe do the mys-
teries of their institution; and to which it has some resemblance
in other respects, particularly having a grand master . . . and in
the non-admission of females. (p. 231)

Each secret society has its own signs and symbols unique to themselves.
The symbols are used by all members to identify themselves and each
other. Since they are considered to be protective in nature, the signs may
be found on clothing, lodges, homes, and even one's body. The Poro
society has five signs: a bunch of leaves, a bundle of twigs, a plume, a
spiral, and two double pyramids placed point-to-point. The pyramids in
particular may be scratched on house walls or drawn in the dirt roads for
members to identify themselves to each other. Often these symbols are
tattooed on the backs of members. Poro also has seven sacred stones that
are important symbols for their rituals. These stones are sacred posses-
sions and must remain in the lodges. As sacred objects they are rarely
seen outside the society enclosures and certainly kept from view of non-
members. Members of Poro also identify themselves through particular
clothing and jewelry. They may even wear objects that they believe hold
power. In this way, the sacred objects act as charms. Big brass toe-rings
are common in identifying Poro men, as are beads.

The Sande is the secret society for women. It, too, has many facets.
The word "Sande" itself may have several meanings. The Sande women
speak of getting Sande from a river or stream. In this way, Sande may be
interpreted to mean a stone or shell that is held sacred by the society. The
word "Sande" may also represent a body of knowledge concerned with
womanly tasks such as child care, homemaking, beauty, the arts, and heal-

ing (Boone, p. 17). Sande may also refer to the organization of women itself, and when any group of initiates meet together, the group is called
Sande. The main Sande symbol is white clay, which is used to paint the
faces of initiates in training. White is the Sande trademark seen in dress
and headgear of its members.

Singing and dancing are essential parts of the Sande school. The history and traditions of the Mande culture are taught through the rhythms,
words, and melodies of songs. The songs and music become mnemonic
devices that help impress cultural lessons on the minds of the young
women (Boone, p. 69). In this way, the Sande cultural history is always remembered and easily passed on. Whether at work or play, song is essential to Sande life.

The Sande initiate is taught "the necessity of singing all through the
day—to keep herself company, to entertain herself, to calm her anxieties,
to keep her mind on amusing and encouraging topics, to pace her movement, to lighten the toil, and help the hours fly . . . songs are a tool, like
a hand or machete, a component of the production process; without songs
it would be literally impossible for Mende to grow crops successfully . . ."
(Boone, p. 71). Many of the songs, as is the tradition, involve the audience
in a "call and response." The Sande use call and response as a method to
evoke and maintain memory. In this way, the music becomes a *lukasa*—a
kind of memory device—as well. Mary Nooter Roberts states it another
way when describing Luba traditions: "music complements a lukasa, then,
as an aural register to a visual model" (Roberts, p. 144). Dance, too, also
an integral part of Sande training, may be considered mnemonic (Nooter,
p. 145). The dance steps themselves become a rhythmic message to be
seen as well as percussively tapped out.

The African symbols of *bogolanfini, nsibidi,* and *vai* employ ideographs—abstract configurations—in conveying messages. They are part of
an African textile tradition in which abstract, figurative, and geometric

designs are used separately, and in combination, to endow the cloth with protective power and to signal information. Because of the bold expressive designs, the cloths can be read quickly and clearly, even from a distance. These visual writing systems are embodied in several cloths. *Adire cloth* consists of blue-on-blue geometric designs made by the Yoruba people of Nigeria using the resist dye method. *Adinkra cloth,* made by the Asante people of Ghana, is associated with mourning rites. It has dark brown or black geometric designs usually stamped on a cream color. *Bogolanfini* cloth, known also as mud cloth because mud is used in creating the designs, is made by the Bamana people of Mali. The cloth usually displays dark brown or black motifs stained on a cream-color fabric. Sometimes the fabric is darkened, leaving the natural light color to form the designs. According to author Tavy D. Aherne, in *Nakunte Diarra: Bogolanfini Artist of the Beledougou,*

> . . . These motifs seem to act as mnemonic devices or cues, which trigger broader reflections about the nature of life and aesthetics. Meanings and names may change or vary from one area and from one artist to another, reflecting a fluid dynamic situation, susceptible to current events and changing concerns. (p. 11)

Regarding the motifs, Aherne references the scholarship of Sarah Catherine Brett-Smith who wrote a 1984 article for *Empirical Studies of the Arts.* In the article, "Speech Made Visible: The Irregular as a System of Meaning," Brett-Smith investigates the meaning of the Bogolanfini motifs. Of the background colors, we know that a rust red is the color of special cloths that indicate membership in a particular society or an elevated status. *Ukara cloth* is a combination of geometric and figurative designs in a dark color on a light background, made by the Igbo people of Nigeria. This cloth belongs to the Leopard Secret Guardian Society. Some of the

Hausa Eight Knives Design

geometric designs include the checkerboard, the pinwheel, and the hour-glass. The figurative designs include the crocodile, the serpent, blacksmith tools, the hand of God, and *nsibidi* symbols. With its many geometric patterns and figurative designs, the *Ukara* cloth resembles a quilt top. Scholars believe the patterns and designs have meaning known only to members of the society.

In the Republic of Benin, the Fon people are renowned for their ap-pliqué banners which are sewn with signs, symbols, and figures represent-ing cultural stories, history of the people, and the accomplishments of the king. The *raffia* cloth of the Kuba people of the Republic of the Kongo is

woven and embellished with embroidery, designs that are abstract ideographs or geometric patterns. Both forms of decoration carry meaning.

Among the textile traditions of Africa is the Hausa embroidery, with
its richly detailed symbolic representations of geography stitched on robes
and shirts. In this symbolic manner, the Hausa embroidered designs serve
as actual maps (see illustration on p. 43).

In addition to the cloths, the *nsibidi* and the *vai* syllabaries are sym-
bolic ideographs, which, like words, depend on context for meaning.
According to Dr. Maude Wahlman, one of the foremost authorities on
African writing systems, there are 690 known *nsibidi* symbols. One exam-

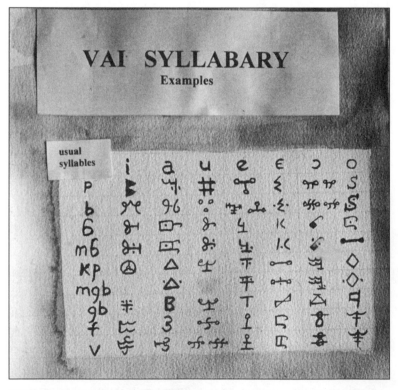

Vai Writing System Modeled After Wahlman

ple of the *nsibidi* is the cross or X design that stands for "word" or "speech." It is a symbol that looks like the Kongo cosmogram depicting the "four moments of the sun," a reference to the cycles of life. The X appears on many objects as well as textiles. The *nsibidi, vai,* and other African writing systems constituted a visual encoded language system evident in many African textiles (see illustrations).

Internationally renowned quilt historian Cuesta Ray Benberry of St. Louis, Missouri, whose thirty-plus years of study and numerous publications introduced the African American quilt with all its complexities to a broad audience of quilt enthusiasts and scholars, writes about the many

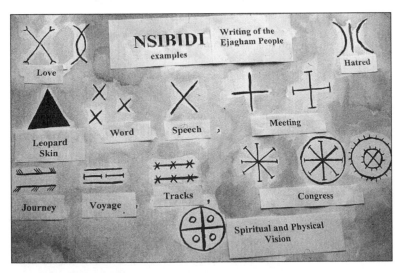

Nsibidi Modeled After Wahlman

ways in which African American quilts are banners of transcendence. In one of her publications, *Always There: The African-American Presence in American Quilts,* Mrs. Benberry traces African American quilt styles from the antebellum period in the South to contemporary quilters in the North. She has argued the case that African American quilts are not limited to any one style, that the "plain" and the "fancy" are both valid African American quilt styles.

Quilt scholar Dr. Gladys-Marie Fry, known for her study of the Harriet Powers Bible quilts and her investigation of slave-made quilts, shows in her book *Stitched from the Soul* how slave quilters pieced precise geometric forms. Her inclusion of several quilts in which there was improvisation within a matrix illustrates the ability of some slave quilters to be creative within a fixed framework.

One such example is the 1860 Tumbling Blocks quilt made by an unknown Alabama slave seamstress. If the illusion of a third dimension is to be achieved, the pattern demands the utmost in precision piecing and color selection. This quilt is similar to many twentieth-century African American quilts in that the fabric choices appear to be the result of improvisation, yet the color selection is very sophisticated (Fry, p. 24) (see color photo section). This one quilt exhibits the two style preferences of many twentieth-century African American quilters: to be respectful of geometric patterns and to be free in choice of fabric and color. Examples of these preferences are seen in photojournalist Roland Freeman's book *A Communion of the Spirits: African-American Quilters, Preservers, and Their Stories*. This book is replete with African American quilts that exhibit precision piecing and a sophisticated use of color, as well as a wide variety of improvisational quilts, some of them bearing striking similarity to African textiles.

Eli Leon is a quilt history researcher made famous by his investigation of African prototypes of the African American abstractly designed, improvised patterns and the strip-piecing technique. In his 1992 catalog *Models in the Mind: African Prototypes in American Patchwork,* he investigates African geometric patterns, their possible meaning, and their relation to African American quilt designs. Subjects of his thought-provoking study are the Half Squares, Nine Patch, Hourglass, Broken Dishes, and

Log Cabin patterns. These geometric patterns and many others carried meaning in Africa and took on added significance within the context of slavery in America.

Leon proffers that the Log Cabin quilt design predates the mid-nineteenth century by several decades and theorizes that the Log Cabin pattern was African in origin. Whether we agree with his theory or not, there exists tangible evidence in the form of linen wrappings of Egyptian mummified humans and animals dating to centuries before the birth of Christ. Dr. Rosalind Jeffries substantiates this by listing the different museums where examples are housed. In her article "African Retentions in African American Quilts and Artifacts," published in *The International Review of African American Art* (Vol. 11, No. 2, 1994), she lists the British Museum, the Cairo Museum, the Metropolitan Museum of Art in New York, and the American Museum of Natural History (see Jeffries, p. 32).

Many African American Log Cabin quilts are a variation of the strict light and dark arrangement of fabric logs around a center square. Many appear to be squares within squares and are fine examples of what has been termed utilitarian quilts. These are the everyday quilts in which large uneven stitches and visible knots add to the rustic charm (see color photo section). Unfortunately, these quilts were often washed in boiling water and lye soap, and as a result, very few if any are still around. We do not count these quilts completely out of the picture, however, because of the quiltmaking custom of using an old tattered quilt as batting for a new quilt.

The geometric-patterned "fancy" quilts have for the most part fared better because they were used less frequently than the utilitarian quilts. Some of the slave-made fancy quilts made their way into the families of slaveholders, only to surface decades later in good shape.

Geometry is not the only element that bears meaning in African American quilts. Abstract, improvised designs, strip-piecing, and bold colors worked in concert to create a visual language and eventually establish an aesthetic choice. One African cultural tie to African American quilts comes in the form of strip quilts. The narrow weave cloths such as *kente* are sewn together in Africa in order to make one piece of fabric. This African technique has long been considered by African art scholars to be the ancestor of African American strip quilts of today.

In both the strip quilt and the string quilt, remnants of fabric are sewn together horizontally one after the other until one long strip of multicolored cloth is made. The strips are then joined together lengthwise to make a quilt top. Often the strips are staggered so that like the African *kente* cloth, the quilt top enjoys a visual rhythm and allows for no straight lines. In the string quilt, the pieces of fabric are very narrow, like ribbons or strings. Both the strip and the string quilt represent a form of improvisational quiltmaking in which color and abstract shapes come together to form a dazzling quilt top.

How could an abstract arrangement of fabric using bold contrasting colors in a quilt top that was either strip-pieced or block-constructed encode anything? Moreover, some of the blocks of patterns were irregular. For example, if the block pattern was a star motif of five points, only three points were completed or the color combination was abruptly changed, effectively creating a broken star. Other African American quilt tops display many different patterns in varying sizes. How might they function? This particular quilt style seemed to glorify confusion.

The bold color contrasts and what would appear on the surface to be poor craftsmanship in piecing fabric into patterns turn out to be the continuation and adaptation of old practices intended to protect the owner as he or she was sleeping. The use of fragmented patterns and the introduction of so many different fabric textures seemed vaguely familiar. It reminded us of the African American cabins wherein the walls were covered with bits of newsprint and torn magazine images. The brilliance of the

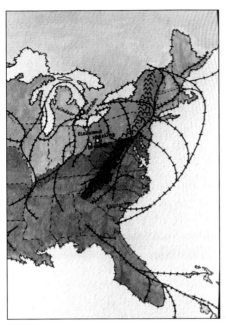

Map illustrating various Underground Railroad escape routes. Created by Christian Harrison, based on a map of the National Park Service, Department of the Interior. (Raymond G. Dobard)

Mrs. Ozella McDaniel Williams in the Charleston Marketplace among her quilts. She holds a wall hanging of the Bear's Paw pattern, a reference, according to the code, to follow the tracks of a bear through the mountains. (Photographed by Raymond G. Dobard)

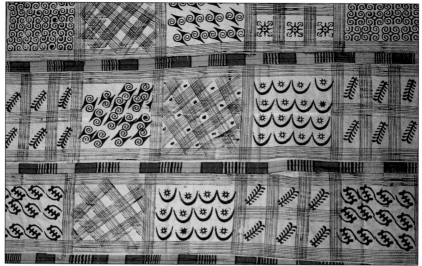

African Andinkra cloth is worn by mourners. Different background colors are associated with various stages of mourning. The patterns are symbols that represent positive elements of life. (Collection/photographed by Kwaku Ofori-Ansa)

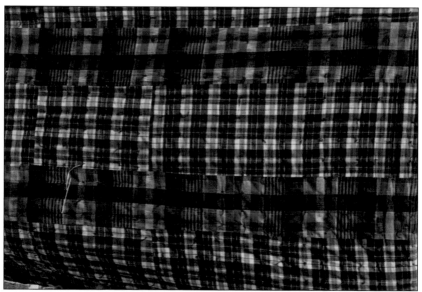

The tied strip quilt is a traditional African American quilt. Note similarities to the Andinkra cloth. Made by Ozella McDaniel Williams. (Collection/photographed by Raymond G. Dobard)

Bogolanfini cloth of the Bamana people of Mali, popularly known in America as mud cloth. Traditionally, only women of noble birth made this cloth. The technique for making Bogolanfini is complicated and believed to be centuries old. Bogolanfini is worn to signify a juncture in life such as marriage, birth, or death. Again, the intricate patterns are symbolic, and the cloth can be read by those familiar with the designs and their context. (Collection/photographed by Raymond G. Dobard)

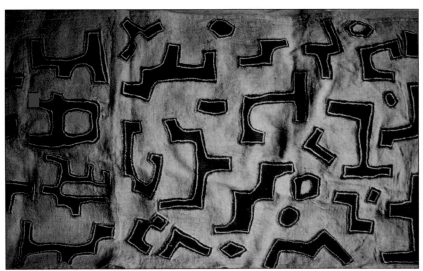

African raffia cloth. The brown patterns compose a secret language or code. The raffia cloth is often used for ceremonial dances. (J. Tobin Collection/photographed by Raymond G. Dobard)

The signature lukasa, or memory board, of the Luba people, Republic of the Kongo, is made from wood, beads, and metal. A lukasa is a board that contains the collective cultural history of a village or society. The beads and metal formulate symbols that can only be read or understood by a chosen few. (See page 38 of Memory: Luba Art and the Making of History *by Mary Nooter and Robert F. Allen.) (Courtesy of the Museum for African Art, New York. Photograph by Jerry L. Thompson)*

The Nine Patch pattern, the simplest quilt pattern to sew, is often the favorite of beginning quilters. This pattern is seen in both African American and Euro-American quilts. (Collection/photographed by Raymond G. Dobard)

This Punu female head mask is used by several ethnic groups, including the Punu, in the Ogowe River area. The design in the middle of the forehead represents scarification marks. The marks bear symbolic meaning to Africans and seem remarkably similar to the American Nine Patch quilt pattern. For the Punu, this mask is known as duma or mvudi and represents a female guardian spirit. (See Masks of Black Africa by Ladislas Segy.) (Collection/ photographed by Raymond G. Dobard)

Iron Wheel motif made by African American blacksmith Philip Simmons. Blacksmithing was an important occupation in Africa. The blacksmith was the keeper of fire and the guardian of culture. The wheel is a rich symbol. In many world cultures it is associated with life cycles and continuity. (Photographed by Raymond G. Dobard)

This large wooden wagon wheel is indicative of many nineteenth-century wagon types and was common to the plantation. This particular example is located on the grounds of the Booker T. Washington Monument in Virginia. (Photographed by Raymond G. Dobard)

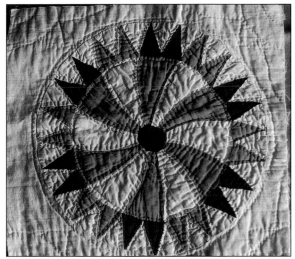

Nineteenth-century example of the Wheel pattern (also known as Wagon Wheel and Blazing Sun). (Collection/ photographed by Raymond G. Dobard)

The Dresden Plate quilt pattern, although named after the prized porcelain plates of Dresden, Germany, is reminiscent of the Wheel pattern and Carpenter's Wheel. We suspect that this pattern was used to indicate the cities of Dresden, Ohio, and Dresden, Ontario, in the code. (Made and photographed by Raymond G. Dobard)

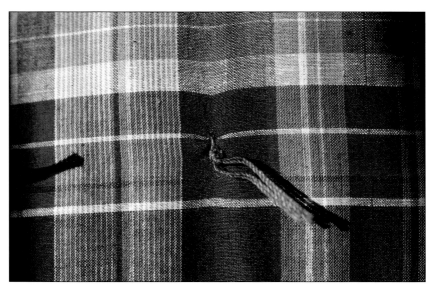

Surface detail of an African American quilt tie made by Ozella McDaniel Williams of Charleston, South Carolina. (Collection/photographed by Raymond G. Dobard)

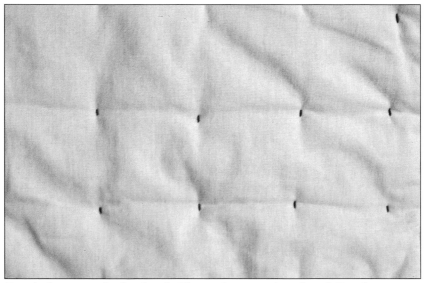

Detail of reverse side of tied quilt. The two-by-two-inch grid was believed to represent a scale, most likely of five- or ten-mile increments—the approximate distance that could be traveled by a slave in a day. Quilt made by Ozella McDaniel Williams of Charleston, South Carolina. (Collection/photographed by Raymond G. Dobard)

quilt top colors could be likened to the flickering of sunlight as it strikes the "bottle tree." Might there be a correlation here? What were the underlying reasons for this aesthetic?

In *Flash of the Spirit,* by Robert Farris Thompson, and in *Drums and Shadows: Survival Studies Among the Georgia Coastal Negroes,* by members of the Georgia Writers' Project of the WPA (1940), we read about the practice in Senegambia that Thompson calls "randomizing the flow of paths" in order to thwart the movement of evil (Thompson, p. 222). The African belief that evil travels in straight lines promoted an African American response in the form of superstitions. Quilts, their decoration, their construction techniques, and their final placement on actual graves all reflect the concern of keeping unwanted evil and/or spirits away.

How is the superstition applied to quilts? According to Thompson and referenced in *Drums and Shadows,* quilt patterns are used in several ways to stop the flow of evil: by breaking patterns within the block unit; by placing different patterns next to one another in a samplerlike fashion; and by staggering designs by using the strip-piecing technique.

Most writers praise the brightly colored quilt top configurations on the basis of style. Rarely would they go any deeper into the possible meaning of the quilt's configuration. Few, if any, have compared the bright colors of the quilts to the attracting and arresting colors of the African American bottle tree.

The African belief is that the realm of the spirit is a realm of bright light, a place of intense reflections. Spirits are instinctively attracted to light. Historian Margaret Washington Creel explains in her book *A Peculiar People* that the Gullahs of the Sea Islands off the coast of Georgia and South Carolina believe in two spirit types—one good and the other troublesome. The good spirit is the heaven-bound spirit. The problem spirit is the "trablin'" spirit. The trablin' spirit is disquieted and roams the land where it once lived, disturbing all there (Creel, p. 317). If the ends of branches of a dead tree are inserted into the neck of empty bottles, preferably blue ones, roaming spirits will be attracted to the bottles when the sun strikes, causing the glass to flash, to glitter. The roaming spirit will then be trapped inside the bottle and rendered harmless to the living. Some believe that the first rays of the morning sun destroy the spirit inside.

Might not the juxtaposition of brightly colored fabric cause the quilt top to appear light-filled and therefore attractive to roaming spirits? We were told on several occasions that different herbs and other objects were placed in the batting, the middle layer of the quilt, in order to give the quilt curative powers. Might not color serve the same purpose?

We know from Thompson, Cheryl Plumer, and others that certain colors and color combinations are considered potent. The combination of red and white, for example, is said to represent the Yoruba god of the storm, Shango. Blue is thought to be a spiritual color. For the Mende and the Ibo, the combination of blue and white is thought to be protective. If this combination is so powerful and so strong in contrast that Thompson compares it to the musical tradition of call and response, is it not conceivable that these colors, whether in textiles/quilts, clothing, or even in architecture, would have been used to signal safety on the Underground Railroad?

Because the color combination of blue and white was popular in mid-nineteenth-century quiltmaking, might not its popularity, its "familiarity," have been a means of hiding the real reason for its use? Is it purely coincidental that blue/white was the color choice for the following patterns: Bear's Paw, Jacob's Ladder, Shoofly, Double Irish Chain, Drunkard's Path, and Monkey Wrench? Should we not consider how color and pattern worked together to encode meaning? Ozella McDaniel Williams did tell us that slaves were able to communicate through the use of color. Whether the colors were bright and many or subdued and few, might not color have complemented geometric as well as abstract forms in conveying messages on the Underground Railroad? And what about stitches? Ozella also told us that stitches formed a visual language.

Most probably the stitches that conveyed hidden meaning would not have been the delicate, barely visible stitches on the fancy geometric-designed quilts. The utilitarian or plain quilts would have been the ideal quilt to use, because the quilting thread was most likely a strong heavy thread. In fact, Ozella said that hemp was used for quilt ties. Hemp, a fiber used to make twine, would be easily visible. The African American utilitarian quilts traditionally had large uneven stitches and bulky quilting knots on the surface of the quilt top. The question to ask is whether the large stitches and knots were an aesthetic choice or an encoded means of communication. These rustic stitches and unsightly knots could always be explained to any inquisitive person because the batting was made from old clothing or a tattered blanket, and it was impossible to make small stitches. Might a matter of practicality have been the perfect disguise? After emancipation and the passing of several generations, the reason for the large stitches and knots was lost, and what remained was the memory that this is the way Grandma did it. We believe it is possible for a covert operation to be the reason for what today is considered an aesthetic choice.

Tracing the threads of the African American quilt took us first to Africa, where we witnessed the cultural spinning of fibers belonging to the secret societies, to secret writing systems, to the talking drums, to encoded textiles, and finally to the fashioning of the African American quilt itself, binding all together, tying, knotting, invoking the blessings of the ancestors.

The Underground Railroad

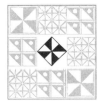

HISTORY IS DEFINED AS A FLOW OF EVENTS OVER TIME. WHO chooses the events to be documented and remembered dictates history. For some time now, the history of the Underground Railroad has been written and told from the point of view of Northern abolitionists, through a romantic rendering of the places and people involved. This romantic rendering told an American story but neglected the African American story. What is missing from this American story is the involvement of the slaves themselves in their own story.

Far from being passive victims waiting to be rescued, enslaved blacks never ceased in their struggle for freedom. From the moment Africans were captured in the interior and coastlands of West Africa, to the time they were sold as slaves in the Caribbean and the new colonies of North America, black slaves acted as aggressively as possible to maintain their own African heritage and seek freedom. Drawing on their cultural strengths and traditions, Africans survived, resisted, and escaped. Their efforts laid the first tracks of the Underground Railroad. But their story, the story of the Underground Railroad from the perspective of the fugitives themselves, has yet to be told.

The story of the Underground Railroad is a part of the much larger story of the personal and cultural survival of these proud African people, brought to America against their will. It is a story that spans the Atlantic, linking forever the peoples of Africa and America. It is a story of places, North and South. It is a story of secrets, involving routes and language, codes and music. It is, in the end, a story of triumph and freedom, bought at great price by individuals, cultures, and countries.

The Underground Railroad has traditionally been thought of as those efforts taken during the peak years of activity, 1830 to 1865, coinciding with the abolitionist movement. But to limit the scope of the story to those years is to focus on only those efforts as recounted by the abolitionists, by some free blacks who kept notes, and by those few slaves who escaped and lived to tell their story. Most fugitive slaves, lacking the skills necessary to read and write, and the resources necessary to "tell their own story" in published form, were forced by circumstances to have accounts of their escape written by sympathetic others, from the perspective of those aiding the fugitives rather than from the perspective of the fugitives themselves.

Little research has been conducted on early efforts of escape and resistance, leading some to conclude that the slave population was "passive" and that slaves waited to act until guided by sympathetic whites. Nothing could be farther from the truth. There is no time during the history of slavery in America that enslaved blacks did not resist, in whatever way circumstances would allow.

The first slaves arrived in Jamestown, Virginia, in 1619. Although initially brought to the new colonies as indentured servants along with their white counterparts, when the Massachusetts colony wrote laws that sanctioned slavery in 1641, the status of blacks changed, thus creating the first distinction of servitude based on race in America. Up until that time it was not unusual to find white and black indentured servants fleeing to freedom together. But when the laws of servitude changed, white indentured servants maintained their status and were allowed eventually to attain their freedom and join society as equals; black indentured servants became slaves with little or no hope of freedom. By 1755 all thirteen colonies had legally recognized slavery as an institution, further ingraining the concept of slavery in America.

The selection of slaves brought to America was not entirely random. Historical documents provide evidence that many plantation owners, without the knowledge necessary to harvest rice, sugar, and indigo, placed specific orders with slave traders to provide Africans already skilled in these areas. The slaves selected were neither uncultured, unskilled, nor heathen. Most came from highly cultured civilizations, from such areas now known as Mali and Senegal, with their own religion, their own traditions, and their own heritage. Many brought skills other than cultivation to the New World: skills in blacksmithing, art, crafts, and textiles. The New World colonies had much to gain from the African presence besides labor. But these skills would remain hidden from the eyes of owners whose perspectives were slanted by racial, economic, and religious beliefs of superiority.

In West Africa, where most of the slave trade was conducted, Senegal's Gorée Island compound was one of fifty slave-holding fortifications punctuating over three hundred miles of the West African coastline. The compound was designed and constructed by European slavers as a holding pen for newly enslaved Africans. Gorée was infamous for its in-

humane treatment and brutal accommodations. It is noted in the diaries
kept by slavers that as many as fifty to sixty children were crammed into
one small cell at a time, sometimes waiting weeks or months for slaving
vessels to arrive. The cells were windowless; the air stagnant; the atmosphere claustrophobic. History documents several slave revolts at Gorée.
In October 1724 fifty-five Africans attempted to break free. With meager
weapons with which to attack, the revolt failed. A frightened child's cries
had given them away.

Children, women, and men held at Gorée were herded through the
corridor and through what was called the Door of No Return. The enslaved Africans were packed into the hulls of ships literally lying side by
side, like spoons, where the stench of sweat, waste matter, and dead bodies was suffocating to all shackled belowdeck. Diseases spread rapidly in
the confined filthy space. It has been estimated that one-fourth to one-half
of the precious "cargo" of black human beings died before reaching a destination in the New World.

While most black slaves became nameless commodities to be bought
and sold, some left their names and their stories to history. One such man
was Olaudah Equiano (1745–97), whose first-person account of his experiences bears witness to the atrocities of slavery.

From Olaudah's memoirs we learn that contrary to popular myth,
slaves did not wait passively to be led out of slavery. From the first moment they were kidnapped from their homeland, shackled and put aboard
ship for the Americas, these Africans plotted their escape. Resistance to
slavery would take many forms, but *it never ceased to occur.* Olaudah speaks
of witnessing suicide among his fellow captives on the slaving vessel.
Many captives tried starving themselves to attain the freedom they sought.
Others tried to band together and stage shipboard revolts. Nearly all
failed in their attempts, but they set the precedent for a resistance movement that can be traced from their first efforts against slavery in Africa

until their descendants were set free in the United States in 1865. Through Olaudah's testimony, African ancestors speak.

Paralleling the slaves' struggle for freedom were the efforts of North American colonists attempting to free themselves from the oppression of English tyranny. In 1776, after the War of Independence, the fledgling nation celebrated freedom. This was a time of ideas, idealism, and acting upon conviction. Appropriately, as the colonists were throwing off their chains of oppression, attention by some turned to the population of slaves also inhabiting this new country. The antislavery movement began in earnest in the North, helped in large part by the religious influence of the Quakers and the economic differences separating the North and the South.

Manumission, the freeing of a slave, was granted to many slaves who had fought in the War for Independence, thus creating a fairly large class of free blacks, both in the North and in the South. Some of these men fought side by side with the colonists out of patriotism to their new country.

Since the 1600s, when slaves were imported by the New England colonies to serve on whalers, fishing boats, and trading vessels, the sea had been home to many black men. These black sailors learned geography, languages, and the customs of others, knowledge that gave them power and caused slave owners fear. Indeed, slave owners had much to fear: These black sailors and shipowners helped many fugitives escape, hiding them aboard ship, and often provided the connecting link for the plantation grapevine that existed between the free blacks up North and their enslaved brethren in the South.

Escaping North American slaves often fled to the swamps, forests, or Spanish colonies in Florida or found sanctuary with the Seminole Indian tribe in Florida. Slaves often knew more about the surrounding areas of plantation lands than their owners and used it to their advantage. Quite often, plantation owners were absentee owners who did not want to live in the more humid, disease-prone climates of the Southern coastal areas. Most large plantation owners lived inland with their families. Thus, renegade slaves were always an issue for whites. Many escaped slaves would later return to the plantation and take revenge on their former owners. Revenge took the form of killing as well as raiding plantations for food, tools, and weapons necessary for survival.

The concern that slave rebellions might cost the slave owners their financial security was very real. In 1787, with the issue of slavery already a foreboding presence in the minds of Northern and Southern citizens, a political compromise was reached to appease both Northern and Southern interests. The Constitution of the United States, recently written, allowed slavery to continue at least until 1808. It also protected involuntary servitude wherever it currently existed. An even more damaging law, the Fugitive Slave Law, was passed in 1793. This law called for the return of any runaway slave. The Fugitive Slave Law and the invention of the cotton gin in 1793 decreased the likelihood that the antislavery movement would prove successful at that time.

The cotton gin enabled Southerners to become the principal supplier of raw cotton for Northern and European textile factories. With slave labor ensuring greater production and profit, all except the enslaved benefited, and slavery as an economically profitable institution became even more entrenched in the South.

In spite of the South's stubborn support for slavery, free blacks in the North continued to press for freedom and attempted to assist their enslaved brothers and sisters. Prince Hall, a free black of Boston, dared to establish a self-help organization. As a manumitted slave, Prince Hall realized that his status as a free black did not allow him total freedom. Free blacks even in the North were still suspect and were subject to codes restricting their access to all the benefits white citizens held. There were few, if any, black schools, black newspapers, or black organizations that would help raise the status of free blacks. Watching carefully as the thirteen colonies of North America expressed their desire for freedom and independence from Britain, Prince Hall decided that he, too, must take action for his cause.

In 1775 Hall decided to apply for membership in the Masonic fraternal organization that attracted so many prestigious thinkers in his day. George Washington and Benjamin Franklin were among the more distinguished and well-known members of Masonic Lodges in their own days. Hall believed that a fraternal organization, such as the Masons, with their tradition of good fellowship and charity, might be just the organization to benefit free blacks. When Hall applied for membership, he was turned down by every Masonic Lodge in America, which then numbered over 150. Not willing to give up, Hall decided to try another route. Finding a British Masonic order that would sponsor them, he and fourteen other blacks were inducted into the British Army Lodge, Number 441. Eleven days later Hall applied for and was granted a permit to establish a separate lodge for blacks. This lodge became the African Lodge and is today known as the Prince Hall Masonic Order. It was the first black Freemasonry Lodge in America. The Prince Hall Masons, a secret fraternal society with secret codes and symbols, would prove to be very helpful in providing cover and secrecy to help enslaved brethren escape to freedom.

There were other examples of free black and white efforts to raise the status and plight of other free blacks. Mutual-benefit societies, such as the African Union Society (begun in 1780) of Newport, Rhode Island, and the African Society (founded in 1796) of Boston, were established to meet the needs of widows and orphans, to provide burial assistance, and to aid in the drafting and execution of wills. In 1787 Richard Allen and Absalom Jones opened the Free African Society as a spiritual haven for

black Philadelphians. Both men were Methodist preachers of African
American ancestry. Rev. Allen would go on to establish the first indepen-
dent black Christian denomination in 1816, the Bethel African Methodist
Episcopal Church. Other black churches, including the first known black
church, the African Baptist or "Bluestone" Church, established in 1758
on the William Byrd Virginia plantation, were essential to the well-being
of both enslaved and free blacks. Self-help and charity toward all were
part of their creed. The churches grew, and with them benevolent societies flourished. One of the early influential black churches was the First
African Baptist Church founded in Savannah, Georgia, in 1788, whose
congregation originally met in barns and arbors.

The black churches during the early days of slavery managed to provide a site where community concerns and projects were planned, right
under the nose of the plantation owner. Learning the language and the rituals of Christianity allowed the slaves to gather together and sing and
speak with words that held one meaning for the masters, another for the
slaves. Many hymns and spirituals were interpreted by the slaves and contained hidden meanings. A great deal of Christian symbols and songs
about the Underground Railroad was conveyed through encoded songs
and became the rallying cry for many a slave in need of persevering grace
and in search of the "promised land."

Denmark Vesey was a former slave in Charleston, South Carolina,
who bought his freedom after winning a lottery. In 1822 Vesey, inspired
by the successful slave uprising by Toussaint-L'Ouverture in Hispanola
years earlier, plotted his own revolt. Vesey was fueled by the knowledge of
this and other slave revolts, the French and American revolutions, and the
debates in Congress over slave and free states' admission to the Union.
Vesey and his followers stockpiled bayonets and daggers and planned a
takeover of a city arsenal, but their plot was revealed by one of the slaves
turned informer. Vesey and thirty-four of his followers were sentenced to

hang but not before information of their actions sent fear up and down the coastal plantations. Their failed effort further fanned the flames of rebellion among plantation slaves everywhere.

On the Sea Islands of Georgia and South Carolina there is still a story told about a boatload of slaves who were originally from the Ibo culture in West Africa. These slaves, in the year 1822, took a look at what awaited them onshore, linked arms, and waded back into the Atlantic saying, "Water brought us and water's gonna take us away." These slaves from Iboland were determined to either walk back to their homeland or die trying. Today, on St. Simons Island, Georgia, a location known as Ibo Landing serves as a reminder to African descendants of these Ibo peoples and of the spirit of resistance inherent in their ancestors.

History tells us that a Kentucky slave named Tice was determined to be free. Fleeing the plantation on which he labored, Tice, like so many other runaways, sought shelter in the woods and on neighboring plantations. He finally made it to the shore of the Ohio River across from the Ripley settlement where many abolitionists lived, including the famous John Rankin and family. With no boat available to him, Tice dove into the chilly water, determined to swim across. The slaveholder followed him in a skiff.

Some writers have suggested that Tice heard the sound of a bell or the call of a bird, one of the local signals indicating that someone was waiting to help him on the other side of the river. Wilbur Siebert, the noted nineteenth-century Underground Railroad historian, writes about the Rankin family and the audio-visual system designed by the people of Ripley, Ohio, to guide runaways to safe shores. Siebert tells us about the whippoorwill birdcalls and the light in the attic window of the Rankin house that stood on the summit of a bluff overlooking the river. With its legendary lighted lantern in the top window, the Rankin house was clearly visible from many miles away in the dark of night. The Rankin house was a lighthouse for those crossing the Ohio River and in desperate need of direction.

Tice probably did not know about the Rankins, but he did know that there were friends on the shoreline of Ohio. The slave owner was within clear sight of Tice, who by then was exhausted, swimming with what little strength he had left. Tice made it to the Ohio shoreline. The slave owner, confidant that he was rapidly gaining on Tice, turned his head away for just one moment. When he looked up, Tice was gone: never to be seen again. The frustrated and somewhat bewildered slave owner declared that Tice had vanished before his very eyes. The slave owner declared it was as if the slave disappeared on some kind of "underground railroad." It was a timely metaphor. What was once the freedom movement eventually became known as the "Underground Railroad" and the "train" would occasionally be nicknamed the "Gospel Train."

In 1871, while most slaves still remained anonymous, William Still, a free black in Philadelphia and a famous Underground Railroad conductor, published interviews of slaves he helped bring to freedom. In 1936, almost a century later, George Rawick compiled former slave interviews under the auspices of the Federal Writers' Project. These interviews are among the few written documentations we have of the life of slavery as narrated by the slaves themselves.

Two examples of individual heroism are well known and stand out in the African American odyssey of courage and action: Harriet Tubman and Frederick Douglass. This black woman and man acted on their desire for liberty or death. John Blassingame refers to Harriet Tubman as a quilter in *Slave Testimony: Two Centuries of Letters, Speeches, Interviews, and Autobiographies*. The reference, an interview which appeared in *The Commonwealth* of July 17, 1863, and corroborated by documents in the Conrad-Tubman Collection of the Schomburg, New York City, states that Tubman engaged in patchwork piecing, sewing small bits of fabric together in order to make quilts (called comforters) for the fugitives in Canada. This Tubman did while hiding in the woods, waiting for the fall of night before continuing her mission northward.

To these two stories we must add the accounts of several white abolitionists, whose active participation distinguished them. Women and men such as the Grimké sisters, originally of Charleston, South Carolina, Lucretia Mott, Levi and Catherine Coffin, John Rankin, Alexander Ross, John Brown, and Thomas Garrett endangered themselves and all they had for the sake of their convictions. All of these ancestors of freedom, both black and white, merit honor in the American story because of their actions, not just their words.

Other active participants in the struggle for freedom were anonymous helpers who belonged to congregations of faith. These included the Quakers, members of the African Methodist Episcopal Church, the Methodist Church, the Presbyterian Church, the Baptist Church, and the African Methodist Episcopal Zion Church. Such religious bodies, as well as the Native American Indians, black benevolent societies and fraternal organizations, and the antislavery societies, worked toward one goal: liberation and self-determination for slaves.

The inspiring accounts of morally principled people who fought a war against injustice enlighten our understanding of the Underground Railroad. Equally illuminating, but more compelling, are the individual stories of heroism and cunning that can still be heard in the families of slave descendants who honor their ancestors with memory. African American elders, understanding the importance of these stories, instruct select family members to commit to memory the stories they tell them. They are then commanded to "pass them on."

Such African American stories have been passed down verbally from generation to generation; few have been written down and brought to light for public scrutiny. Some have found their way into children's books, but the majority have remained in the realm of oral history, which is often discounted and ignored by historians writing the history of America. A shroud of secrecy and the lack of written texts continue to thwart efforts to document these stories.

The stories are crucial to our understanding of the early striving for freedom by blacks enslaved in America. Since they lacked the ability to read or write a language foreign to them, enslaved in a country they knew nothing about, where the color of their skin set them apart from others and determined their status, we must ask the questions that have yet to be answered: How did slaves plan their escape? What skills and knowledge did these black men and women possess to aid them? Whom could they trust when even persons of their own skin color had been turned into part of the conspiracy to keep them enslaved? How would they take the first steps off the plantation and where would they go?

Leaving the plantation was a life-or-death decision for the slaves. Clothed only in whatever would not draw attention and with only the food and tools they could carry with them, escaping slaves traveled miles by foot. The journey required planning, skills, knowledge, and luck. Most early efforts were conducted by their own design and required the utmost secrecy. The nature of secrecy necessary for escape meant that little was ever put to paper. Since it was the law that slaves were not allowed to be taught to read or write, other methods were needed to ensure successful efforts for escape. Most information regarding escape had to be committed to memory and passed on only by word of mouth, using codes, signs, and signals created by slaves and shared only with those who could be trusted.

The plantation grapevine was well known to white planters, who feared communication among blacks. Laws were passed to curtail such communication, including laws preventing the education of blacks, the congregating of blacks unless supervised by whites, and drumming, since it was feared to be a means of secret communication brought over from Africa. Laws could not curb this communication grapevine, however. The means of secret communication and secret slave gatherings just went further underground. Slaves were required to become more devious and creative in their methods. "Puttin' on the Massa" became a favorite way of creating a false security for whites.

The plantation grapevine was more than just casual communication. History documents an extraordinary means of communication connecting free blacks in the North and South with their enslaved brethren. In his thought-provoking book *Free People of Color: Inside the African American Community,* James Oliver Horton presents archival testimonies that indicate there was an "interregional communication system" existing between free blacks of the Northeast, the Midwest, and the South and enslaved Southern blacks. Horton chronicles how enslaved blacks and free blacks were able to meet at inns frequented by traveling plantation owners who were accompanied by black slaves acting as drivers and servants. He discusses how black sailors were able to exchange information with enslaved blacks at port cities; how slaves who were hired out to shops were able to gather information; how the black churches, even under the scrutiny of whites, acted as "post offices" for messages containing escape routes and instructions for escape and survival; and how plantation slaves hired out to work in a neighboring town served as dispatchers of these messages.

From Horton and the scholarship of others whom he cites, we learn about the close ties binding the free black community in the North to enslaved blacks in the South, quite often family members trying to stay in touch. The black community, North and South, had devised a system of transmitting information, many times in coded form, to their own. Sending and receiving such information would happen right in the open, in churches and other gatherings such as quilting bees and husking parties.

Because members of the free black network, most of whom were liter-
ate, were able to compile facts regarding geography, landmarks, places to
avoid, obscure trails, mileage, and the locations of safe places where food
and rest were waiting, many escaping slaves knew where to go and how to
get there. Former runaways shared their own tactics and routes of escape.
Most early escape attempts were individual efforts by slaves, not part of any
organized cooperative ventures headed by Northern abolitionists. Their escapes blazed the trails that later became the Underground Railroad.

The Underground Railroad is the continuation of this compelling
story of resistance and struggle of slaves in their quest for freedom, incorporating every route, every person, every place, and every act taken by
or on behalf of the enslaved. The Underground Railroad story spans the
Atlantic, stretching from the interior villages of Central Africa to the
coastal kingdoms of West Africa; from Senegal in the north to Angola in
the south; stretching across the Atlantic Ocean to the New World plantations in the Caribbean and North and South America. It is a story dating back to the 1400s when the Portuguese landed in what is now known
as Sierra Leone and began the first mass enslavement and movement of
Africans to the Western Hemisphere. It is the story of slave traders,
white, Arab, and black, and the Africans they enslaved. It is the story of
families torn asunder, kidnapped, bought, and sold. It is the story of individuals choosing their destiny. It is the story of a people's struggle for
freedom echoed in the words of Harriet Tubman and Frederick Douglass
declaring their intentions to "live free or die."

By virtue of its covert nature, the Underground Railroad is also the
story of codes and secrets involving cunning systems of visual and oral
communication, known only to those involved and reflecting the in-
domitable spirit of a people's resistance to slavery and desire to be free.

While we know little about the methods slaves used to avoid detection
when leaving the plantation, we know that codes were used. In memoirs

left by Alexander Ross, a Canadian abolitionist and noted ornithologist, we learn how he used his scientific skill to help slaves connect with the Underground Railroad once they reached the border states. Ross is credited with devising an elaborate mathematical code to assist slaves in leaving the plantation and traveling north to freedom. There were other codes as well, spirituals, forms of dance, and symbols committed to memory. Some codes were designed and used by whites aiding the fugitives; other codes were designed and used by the slaves. Whether lost to time, secrecy, or by design by those who feared disclosure, history has documented only a few.

Now, recently revealed, is one of those secret codes designed by slaves. Used before the more popular dates of the Underground Railroad, this code, named the Underground Railroad Quilt Code, led many to freedom.

The Quilt Code gives us access to some of the secrets still remaining about the early years of escape from the plantations. It allows us to see how ingenious were these fugitives in crafting their own escape. The code confirms the use of quilts as visual maps to freedom.

Forging a link between the past and the present, between Africa and America, between blacks and whites, and a route from the South to the North, Mrs. Ozella McDaniel Williams, a modern-day griot from South Carolina, reveals a story, the story told to her by her mother and grandmother before her, the story of the Underground Railroad Quilt Code. With the telling comes the responsibility to honor these African American ancestors, not just as slaves but also as masters of their own destiny.

"There are five square knots on the quilt every two inches apart. They escaped on the fifth knot on the tenth pattern and went to Ontario, Canada."

Chapter Three

"There Are Five Square Knots..."

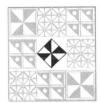

BECAUSE OF ITS IMAGERY, OZELLA'S UNDERGROUND RAILROAD Quilt Code lends itself to conjecture. Exactly how the code was used, we do not know. However, Ozella's words and our research enable us to theorize the following. The quilt patterns listed in the code were intended as mnemonic devices. They were used to aid the slaves in memorizing directives before leaving the plantation. The names of quilt patterns function as metaphors in the code; in other words, the patterns represent certain meanings.

When Ozella first revealed the code to Jacki, she instructed her to write down the numbers one through ten. She then listed nine patterns and one phrase: Monkey Wrench, Wagon Wheel, Log Cabin, Shoofly, Bow Ties, Cathedral Church, Double Wedding Rings, Flying Geese, Drunkard's Path, and Tumbling Boxes. Then Ozella recited the code.

However, the code she recited also included the following quilt pattern names: Bear's Paw, Crossroads, and Stars (North Star).

Why were they excluded from the original list? We can explain.

According to Ozella, there were ten quilts used to direct the slaves to take particular actions. Each quilt featured one of the ten patterns. The ten quilts were placed one at a time on a fence. Since it was common for quilts to be aired out frequently, the master and mistress would not be suspicious when seeing the quilts displayed in this fashion. This way, the slaves could nonverbally alert those who were escaping. Only one quilt would appear at any one time. Each quilt signaled a specific action for a slave to take at the particular time that the quilt was on view. Ozella explained that when the Monkey Wrench quilt pattern was displayed, the slaves were to gather all the tools they might need on the journey to freedom. The second quilt placed on the fence was the Wagon Wheel pattern, which signaled the slaves to pack all the things that would go in a wagon or that would be used in transit. When the quilt with the Tumbling Boxes pattern appeared, the slaves knew it was time to escape. How long each quilt remained on the fence before being replaced is not known. Ozella suspected that a quilt would remain up until all who were planning to escape had completed the signaled task. The code had dual meaning: first to signal slaves to prepare to escape and second to give clues and indicate directions on the journey.

We strongly believe that in order to memorize the whole code, a sampler quilt was used. The sampler quilt would include all of the patterns arranged in the order of the code. Traditionally the sampler quilt was used to teach pattern piecing. Think of it as a book of fabric patterns. If the mistress or anyone saw the griot conducting a class on patterns, praise for industrious behavior would be the outcome. No one would suspect what was really taking place.

Together, the quilt patterns as metaphors and as signs instructed the escaping slaves on how to prepare for escape, what to do on the journey, and where to go. The quilt patterns worked in conjunction with spirituals and topographical stitching to create a map in the mind of those escaping.

There are two different ways to put quilts together: knotting and stitching. To a plantation mistress who was familiar with the traditional Euro-American quilts, a quilt with the knots left visible on the front was the result of shoddy and hasty workmanship, but the slaves knew better.

According to Ozella, the first two quilts the seamstress displayed would have ties with only one square knot on each tie. The next two displayed, quilts three and four, would have two square knots on each. Quilts five and six had three, and quilts seven and eight had four. Quilts nine and ten would have five square knots on each tie. The tenth quilt pattern, however, identified by her as the Tumbling Boxes or Tumbling Blocks, was distinguished by virtue of its being number ten and bearing five knots. Ozella proposed that the Tumbling Boxes pattern was chosen to be the final pattern because of the association between boxes and "packing up and moving on." She said that when the Tumbling Boxes quilt was displayed on the fence, supposedly to be aired, that was the signal to box all one's belongings, pack them, and move on, or to escape. We cannot help but question why five square knots? Why not six or four? Why were five square knots on pattern nine? Why not reserve the five square knots for pattern ten? Obviously there is significance in the number five. There had to be more to this numbering-knotting system. We had to find out.

We suspected that tying knots could be related to African rituals, but how is it manifested in quiltmaking? For that matter, how does tying work? After a quilt top was pieced, instead of stitching together the quilt top with the batting and the backing, the slaves used twine to join the quilt together with simple ties (see color photo section). The ties were usually placed several inches apart and were knotted on the front, or the top, of a quilt. Ozella was clear in telling us that the ties were placed two inches apart and were used to hold the batting in place. She also made it clear that each tie would be made of a certain number of knots.

Making twine ties on a quilt top is similar to tying a bow on top of a gift box. Instead of making a bow out of the twine, the quilter makes several knots: usually square knots, to secure the layers of the quilt as well as to ensure that the twine does not unravel. As far as the quilt described in the Quilt Code was concerned, the top of the quilt had *"five square knots on the quilt every two inches apart."* That is, the quilt top had ties placed every two inches apart, and each tie was composed of square knots. This created a grid-like pattern on the back of the quilt.

We could appreciate how the quilt was constructed, but we still couldn't figure out why the code specified that *five* knots would be needed to tie together a regular quilt, when it seemed that one or possibly two knots would suffice. We were determined to find out.

While researching references to Underground Railroad codes, we discovered Alexander Ross, a Canadian Mason who was by profession an ornithologist and by conviction an abolitionist. Ross is credited with inventing his own code, which he personally used to assist slaves in their flight to freedom. Ross brought several assets to bear. First of all he was Canadian and therefore familiar with Canadian terrain and the many routes leading there. Second, Ross made numerous trips to the South in the late 1850s, thereby gaining firsthand knowledge of potential escape routes. Last but by no means least, he was a respected white scientist whose study of birds gave him access to the Southern gentry social circles and thus to the plantations.

We assumed that Ross entertained his hosts with his encyclopedic knowledge of birds, and with their permission, roamed the grounds of the plantation freely conducting his research without supervision. Without the knowledge of his Southern hosts, however, Ross was interested not only in birds and geese, but in the *flight of slaves* as well. Once he was able to determine whom he might trust among the slave population, he was able to impart his escape plans. Since he recorded making several trips between Canada and the South, we believe that Ross had directions to Southern safe houses as well as those in the North.

The Ross code used numbers, pious praises, and the times of day to instruct slaves in running away. He identified the number and the gender of the fugitives by referring to them as "hardware" for males or "dry goods" for females. These were the "packages" in the Ross system. The Ross code is cited most notably in the work of Henrietta Buckmaster. The Ross code, like the Underground Railroad Quilt Code, was predicated upon memory. Once the key was committed to memory, only the initiated would be able to discern the message hidden in what would appear to be a simple note or letter. Ross utilized numbers and poetic descriptions in formulating his code. We are told that Pennsylvania was recognized as number 10; Seville, Ohio, was number 20; Medina, Ohio, was number 27; Cleveland, Ohio, was called "Hope"; Sandusky, Ohio, was known as "Sunrise," and Detroit, Michigan, was dubbed "Midnight." The entryways into Canada were designated by words of praise and thanksgiving to the Almighty: "Glory to God" meant Windsor, Ontario, and "God be praised" stood for Port Stanley (Buckmaster, p. 249). As such, one proposed message reads: "We hope to rise at sunrise; then we will rest by midnight" (Hamilton, *Many Thousand Gone*, p. 117). Translated, the message states: Cleveland to Sandusky to Detroit. The final destination was Ontario ("Glory to God and God be praised"). Buckmaster and others missed a probable reference to the Buxton-Chatham area in Canada where several early black settlements existed, and where John Brown, Frederick Douglass, and Harriet Tubman gathered for meetings. One notable settlement was called the Dawn settlement, founded by Josiah Henson in the early 1800s, located slightly northeast of Detroit, near Dresden, Ontario.

In addition to discussing Canadian cities, Alexander Ross cites Cincinnati, Sandusky, Toledo, Cleveland, and other cities in Ohio as meeting places, points of departure and safe houses in his published account of his activities as an abolitionist (see Ross, *Recollections and Experiences*).

Wilbur Siebert and other Underground Railroad scholars write that safe houses or resting places were usually between five and twenty-five miles apart. Siebert's 1898 study of Underground Railroad activity in the state of Ohio has proved to be seminal to all subsequent studies. This Ohio State University professor emeritus of history painstakingly charted all known routes, cited all cities and townships that were involved in Underground Railroad activity, and disclosed the names of individuals as well as pinpointing their houses. As a result of his thoroughness, Siebert was able to emphatically state that the number and location of safe houses created a pattern that resembled a net, and that "zigzag was one of the regular devices [used] to blind and throw off pursuit" (Siebert, 1898a, p. 62). In his publication regarding the early years of the Underground Railroad, Siebert indicates that five miles or multiples of five was the norm in Ohio. Could the Quilt Code be referring to the distance between safe houses?

Ross, Siebert, and certainly the network of houses and stations in Ohio are reason enough to suspect that the grid and the numbers in the Quilt Code are mapping indicators, providing a scale for mileage, for the distances between safe houses. We felt that there was more to it, however. We continued to look for the missing piece to the puzzle.

Ross, like Siebert and other nineteenth-century writers, records free blacks as "agents" on the Underground Railroad. The help of free black communities and benevolent societies in Cleveland and especially Sandusky are well documented as vital to the success of the Underground Railroad. Given the number of black secret, charitable and fraternal organizations that were active in promoting freedom, we gave careful consideration to any possible links between fraternal or other secret societies' secret signs and symbols and the Quilt Code. We looked specifically at the Masons. We learned of someone called a fellowcraft, a Masonic initiate who's still learning the craft and is given a cable tow, a length of knotted rope that is a symbol of his commitment to the lodge and the community. The cable tow is also a means of measurement, a symbolic indicator of the distance the fellowcraft is willing "to travel" for the lodge. The cable tow is knotted in correlation to a level of achievement, usually three, five, or seven knots indicate rank. Since the square is one of the major Masonic emblems, might the number five and the designation "square," as in "five square knots," suggest a mathematical system invented by the Prince Hall Masons in order to assist their enslaved brethren? With the wealth of information that is now being published about the involvement of the free black community in the fight against slavery, there is more than ample reason to suspect that a Prince Hall Mason may have influenced the Quilt Code.

Having learned the relevance of numbers and knots in Masonic coding, we then investigated the African tradition of knotting as a ritual act and as a means of transmitting messages.

One prominent African example in which knotting has a hidden significance is the *nkisi makolo* in the Kongo. A *nkisi* is a charm; while the *nkisi makolo* refers to a particular charm in which knots *(makolo)* are used. In this tradition, the tying and knotting empower an object. In his seminal work on African and African American art, *Flash of the Spirit,* Robert Farris Thompson draws our attention to the importance of tying and knotting in the Kongo culture. According to Thompson, the Bakongo people of the Kongo made power objects such as *minkisi* (the plural of *nkisi*). Professor Thompson tells us that *minkisi* containers vary greatly in form—from shells, to packets, bags, and cloth bundles—and that tying knots is integral to the making of many *minkisi.* Thompson frequently cites African culture specialist Dr. Fu-Kiau Benseki regarding the Bakongo tradition of tying a certain number of knots. Dr. Benseki links the number of knots to an African ritual mathematical system. He explains that the knots are used as incantations and therefore contain power.

The Bakongo tradition of tying knots in the making of *minkisi* enables us to consider the five square knots placed two inches apart in the code to be a means of making the quilt into a *nkisi,* an object possessing protective power.

A trip to an African textile shop of a former Howard University graduate student provided a fascinating explanation. Mrs. Gihgi Ogbonna, who once taught African textiles at the University of Nigeria, described to us what the five square knots meant according to her own Ibo tradition. Similar to the way in which a rosary is not complete until all five decades have been recited, the tying of the knots is performed in ritual fashion and is used to empower, invoke the ancestors, and protect and guide.

When showed Ozella's Quilt Code, Mrs. Ogbonna said she understood why the five square knots were used on the quilts. The knots were to invoke the protection of the ancestors and Almighty God for those going on a journey. Thus, not only did the five knots most likely indicate distance on a map, but they were also a symbol of protection for the departing slaves.

Scholar Elizabeth Dornan and others have documented the fact that large numbers of the Nigerian Ibo tribe were brought to Charleston to work as slaves. A similar knotting tradition has also been traced to Angola and today's Republic of the Kongo, again, a region from which many enslaved Africans were transported to South Carolina.

We suggest that the five square knots are there as protective invocations commending the departing slaves to the care of the ancestors and the help of communities outside the plantation. Although the ties with their five square knots also served a practical need by creating a grid by which the distance between safe houses could be measured, the knots communicated much more to the slave community. Those heading out on a long and uncertain journey would know that they were spiritually tied to the many loved ones they'd have to leave behind—with very little expectation of seeing them again in this world.

When we think of the knots and the Ibo tradition, we see how ordinary things assumed extraordinary meanings, how the knots invoking protection and sustaining connections were hidden in plain view. Communicating secrets by using ordinary objects is very much a part of African culture, in which familiarity provides the perfect cover. Messages can be skillfully passed on through objects that are seen so often that they become invisible. Knots are merely knots to the uninitiated. A string of knots or beads numbering ten and repeated five times with a space and a single bead in between appears to be a decorative arrangement. However, make a circle out of this sequence of beads and spaces and add a bead, a space, three beads, a space, and a cross, and you have a rosary: a devotional object intended to foster prayer and meditation for millions of Roman Catholics. To people not of the Catholic faith, the arrangement of beads would mean nothing without the cross. The same example is true of Tibetan prayer beads or those used in Islam. Unless an individual knows what to look for, the beads will seem only decorative. And so it was for the quilts that were used in the Underground Railroad Quilt Code.

The members of an African secret society called the Kufong, like the Masonic initiate the fellowcraft, also communicate with one another using knots. During a conversation, a member of this society makes a series of knots on a string or vine. If the person with whom he is speaking is also a member of the society, the person would recognize the pattern of knots and would respond by adding an answering knot. Again, this is one of several ways in which secret society communication systems function through the use of ordinary objects. In addition, stones, grains of corn, peppers, charcoal, folded materials, and cowrie shells also form the script for visual languages (Butt Thompson, pp. 167–70).

Communication in secretive form also existed in quilt stitches. Ozella once stated that the stitches on the quilt formed a language that the slaves used to aid their escape. She first made this disclosure in 1993 while pointing directly to a quilt covered with traditional quilt stitches.

The first-person remembrances of quilter octogenarian Mrs. Elizabeth

Talford Scott, who grew up in Chester, South Carolina, and her daughter Joyce helped us understand how quilt stitches could be used to make a map. Like a quilt, Mrs. Scott's story is multilayered. Both she and her daughter are well known quilters. Mrs. Scott is famous for her quilts, which, according to several publications, display elements of design and construction methods that are African in origin. Her quilts are frequently distinguished by the rocks, beads, and amulets that are sewn to the quilt top. Leslie King-Hammond, a specialist on African American art, a personal friend of the Scotts', and dean of the Maryland Institute of Art, compares the beads, knotted fabric, and rocks found on Mrs. Scott's quilts to the beads and other objects attached to the *lukasa,* the memory boards of the central African Luba people.

The *lukasa,* or memory board, is a mnemonic device used by members of the highest level of Luba royal association. The *lukasa* contains secret mythical, historical, genealogical, and medicinal knowledge. Beads on the front of the board are positioned in such a way (and in different colors) as to communicate a list of kings, proverbs, and praise phrases. Engraved geometric patterns on the back codify the secret prohibitions relating to kingship. The tablet serves to recall aspects of Luba history, while at the same time allowing for its creative reinterpretation.

Thus, the memory boards are in the same category with encoded textiles, sculptures, and other objects bearing information. With the *lukasa* as well as the textiles, secrets are communicated indirectly. There is no one-to-one correlation of sign and signified; according to African art scholars Mary Nooter Roberts and Allen F. Roberts, readings may change, depending on the setting, the participants, and the text's purpose. And the secrets themselves are always changing, for they depend on social context.

Some *lukasa* may be sculpted or inscribed although mostly beads are used. *Lukasas* do not symbolize thought as much as stimulate it. Thus for the Luba and for the Greeks, the concepts of remembering and forgetting are linked. The *lukasa* allows for the forgetting of facts or the omission of facts and the remembering of them or others depending on who is "reading" the object. The Greeks called these concepts Lethe (forgetting) and Mnemosyne (memory) (Nooter Roberts and Roberts, *Memory*, pp. 44–47). In today's world we have the computer chip that stores our data in memory banks. In relating the *lukasa* to a computer, Dr. King-Hammond related an encounter she had with a child at the Museum of African Art.

Dr. King-Hammond told us that as she was leading a group of eight- to twelve-year-old school children through the Luba exhibition, she stopped at the *lukasa* and asked if anyone could identify the art object. Much to her astonishment a little boy of about eight years old answered, saying, "It's a computer. I bet you can read it." The innocent yet informed eye of a child who has been exposed to the abstract languages of computers instantly understood what scholars have been studying for years. Needless to say, his response quickly ended Dr. King-Hammond's lecture. As she explained, what more could she possibly add?

Dr. King-Hammond could, however, articulate the meaning and methodology of the Elizabeth Scott quilts and stressed how Mrs. Scott was continuing an African tradition as interpreted in the creation of all of her quilts. In a manner similar to the Luba *lukasa*, Mrs. Scott employs the rocks, knots, and other objects to activate memory.

Mrs. Scott also conveys messages through her stitches. Her testimony that stitches were used by slaves to draw a map of the plantation sounds similar to the claim of Ozella that the length and position of the stitches formed a language that only the slaves knew. The use of stitches and knots, as a form of communication, a kind of Morse code in thread, along with fabric color and quilt patterns, made it possible to design a visual language.

According to Mrs. Scott, whose grandfather was a former slave, "Slave quilts tell a story." She says that the style of stitching on a quilt would differ from family to family, as determined by the family's place of origin. Each family would pass on a distinctive stitching style to the next generation. Mrs. Scott relates a story about a certain "plantation quilt" she once owned. She says that this quilt was plain, with a white base, and that rows of stitches on it represented the rows of crops on the plantation, forming what her daughter, Joyce, calls a topographical map of the plantation.

Mrs. Scott replicated this quilt from memory in her 1980 Plantation Quilt, in which stars are the main theme (see color photo section). The central "shootin' " star is surrounded by intricate stitching and heavy quilting. The congested lines of quilt stitches simulate the contours of the farm fields. Joyce notes that it is an example of an African American genre of map quilts. She goes on to say in the *Stitching Memories* quilt show catalog: "My mother was told . . . that slaves would work out a quilt piece by piece, field by field, until they had an actual map, an escape route. And they used that map to find out how to get off the plantation" (Grudin, p. 32).

Remembering her childhood, Mrs. Scott tells us that the quilting bees were for women *and* men. In certain parts of Africa, past and present, men have played an integral part in textile design: even in the making of "fabric armor," quilted war shirts and horse armor by the Fulani (in fact, the kente cloth popular today has traditionally been woven by men). The kids, she explains, would sit underneath the quilting frame, and listen to the older relatives' stories. On one of those occasions, Mrs. Scott remembers, a family member said, "This is where your cousin would pick cotton." Another family member, pointing to a different place on the quilt, responded, "No, it was farther to the left." Her family was clearly making reference to the quilt as a map of the plantation.

The Scott family tradition of rendering the plantation layout by primarily using stitches is not without precedent in Africa. Several nineteenth-century African examples indicate how textiles were used to "map" geographical sites (see color photo section). The Hausa of Nigeria are well known for their exquisite embroidery, and a layout of the chieftain's village is often presented in what appears to be abstract geometric form (Kiewe, p. 579). In Muslim West Africa the pattern is known as Eight Knives and contains stylized renderings of the chieftain's house, the mosque, and other structures. The central motif is similar to the Nine Patch quilt pattern, which the Hausa call "five houses" or "house of five." Here, too, the number five is significant. In *Models in the Mind,* Eli Leon cites the work of Colleen Kriger, who in a 1988 article, "Robes of the Sokoto Caliphate," published in *Africa Arts,* states that the number five was a talisman to guard against the evil eye (Leon, p. 15). The Hausa embroidery is an early African example of using textiles to map geographical sites (see color photo section).

Whether the five square knots on the quilt is a Hausa charm, an Ibo invocation, Bakongo power ties, a Masonic symbol, or reference to the Underground Railroad web of safe houses in Ohio, one thing is certain: The number five is symbolic in African and African American cultures.

According to Ozella, the five square knots appeared on the tenth pattern, which was the Tumbling Boxes pattern, also known as Tumbling Blocks and Baby Blocks. The pattern is an old one, dating back at least to the early nineteenth century. A fine example of a slave-made Tumbling Blocks quilt can be found in Dr. Gladys-Marie Fry's *Stitched from the Soul* (p. 24). This pattern demands precise piecing if the corners are to meet perfectly and the illusion of three dimensions achieved. Obviously, the Quilt Code seamstress, like the unknown Alabama slave seamstress whose work is featured in Dr. Fry's book, had to have been a very fine craftsperson indeed. This is further proof that the bulky knots and unusual stitching found on some of the tied quilts of the Quilt Code was certainly intentional. With the display of this quilt on the fence, the slaves knew the time had arrived to box up and move on. They were to look to a mysterious someone referred to in the next chapter as The Monkey Wrench.

"The monkey wrench turns the wagon wheel toward Canada on a bear's paw trail to the crossroads."

C h a p t e r   F o u r

"The Monkey Wrench Turns the Wagon Wheel . . ."

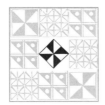

OZELLA TOLD US THAT A QUILT MADE OF MONKEY WRENCH patterned blocks was the first of the ten quilts displayed as a signal for those slaves who planned to escape. (See color photo section.) She said the Monkey Wrench quilt was a signal for the slaves to begin their escape preparations by collecting the "tools" they thought they would need on their journey north. We may interpret the word "tools" to mean several kinds of implements: some for constructing physical shelters, some for determining directions like compasses, or others for defending oneself. Alexander Ross writes that he gave escaping slaves a compass, a knife, some food, and a few coins to aid them on their journey. In addition, there were the mental tools: cunning, alertness, the ability to discern motives of strangers, and knowledge. These would complement any common tools and would complement the entire undertaking. The money wrench was an essential tool in transforming metal; mental tools could be used to transform the slave, to reshape self-images. Knowledge has always been the most effective tool no matter what the situation. It is possible that "gathering tools" was a coded expression admonishing the slaves to be prepared on all levels, especially on the mental one.

Ozella went on to clarify for us the meaning of the wagon wheel, the bear's paw trail, and the crossroads. She said that the Wagon Wheel quilt, the second one to be displayed on the fence, was a sign alerting the slaves to pack provisions for their journey as if they were packing a wagon, meaning that they should think about what was essential for survival during their trip. Ozella also addressed the bear's paw trail, explaining that it was really a visual reference reminding the fugitives to follow the actual trail of a bear's footprints. These footprints would undoubtedly indicate the best path and would also lead to food and/or water. She further explained that the fugitive party appropriated quiltmaking language to help them identify their paths. One example she gave was in the use of the term "trip around the world," the name of a quilt pattern the fugitives used to indicate a path around a mountain instead of over it. She told us that if anyone—overseer, master, or mistress—overheard the slaves talking about taking a trip around the world, they would have dismissed it as gibberish.

Once the slave party made it through the mountains, they were to travel to the crossroads. Ozella made it abundantly clear that Cleveland, Ohio, was the main crossroads.

When we interpreted this passage of the code, we were able to appreciate and to augment what Ozella said. We began with a close look at the term "monkey wrench" and considered it within its American and African cultural context. We then focused on the possible meaning of the wagon wheel, suspecting that it stood for the fugitive party. When we turned to the bear's paw trail, we realized that the reference was specific

to the Appalachian mountain range because the Appalachian range was
the closest to the South Carolina area, and ran along a southwest to northeast axis that paralleled charted Underground Railroad routes. Our last
consideration in this sentence of the code was the city of Cleveland, sin-
gled out by Ozella and some historians as a major terminal on the
Underground Railroad, a port to Canada, and the crossroads.

Detail of the Nigerian Ukara Cloth. Note Monkey Wrench at Bottom

On the plantation, the monkey wrench was a tool used primarily by
the blacksmith, since there were no plumbers during slavery. In Africa,
too, the monkey wrench was used primarily by the blacksmith and was
therefore an honored tool.

On the Nigerian Ukara cloth, belonging to the African Leopard
Secret Guardian Society, the monkey wrench appears in a square with

other tools that scholars like Rosalind Jeffries have linked to the African blacksmith (Jeffries, p. 28) (see illustration). Several scholars, including Patrick R. McNaughton, inform us of the privileged role the blacksmith enjoyed within his community because of his talents and knowledge. We are told that blacksmiths often headed male secret societies, such as the Poro Society of the Mende people. In addition, the Mende blacksmith was the community's medical advisor as well as a sculptor. He was the

Anvil in Philip Simmon's Studio

keeper of fire and the one who knew how to configure metal and to metaphorically shape society.

In America, the skill of African American blacksmiths has long been respected by both the black and the white communities. In the antebellum South intricate wrought-iron work was linked to the owner's wealth and prestige. The greater the amount of wrought iron on a house, the greater the prestige and perceived wealth of the owner. To this day, the association between wealth and wrought-iron enhancement continues.

Today, no one would question the respect and honor the art world has bestowed upon Philip Simmons, a well-known African American blacksmith of Charleston, South Carolina. But what about the blacksmith on the plantation during the time of slavery? Was he considered a mere laborer, albeit skilled, by the plantation owner? We suspect that the plantation blacksmith was the dispatcher of information using the anvil and hammer to ring out messages, as his predecessors did in Africa. Did the anvil, hammer, and bellows replace the talking drums when they were outlawed? We believe that the blacksmith was able to "talk" to his community through his rhythmic hitting of hammer to anvil and through the sounds produced by the bellows. The blacksmith was probably a major source of information and an adept communicator. When "loaned out" to other plantations, he used the opportunity to collect geographical information. His cleverness and importance were hidden under the guise of strenuous hard labor where sweat tempered metal. We suggest that the blacksmith was probably one of the masterminds who helped plan the escapes and that the monkey wrench might be a reference to him. But we think the monkey wrench had other meanings as well.

The Monkey Wrench, also called the Double Monkey Wrench, is one of several nineteenth-century American quilt patterns named after a trade or occupation. Others include Anvil, Circular Saw, Carpenter's Wheel, Carpenter's Square, and Square and Compass. The Monkey Wrench pattern is celebrated for its striking simplicity, an arrangement of rectangles, right triangles, and squares. The pattern name conjures images of a heavy metal tool, a craft, and strong, knowledgeable hands. The monkey wrench turning the wagon wheel implies that the wrench, whoever or whatever it might have been, exercised authority over the wagon wheel. The monkey wrench had to be a person or group of people, an organization perhaps, who had access to the plantation, was familiar with its daily operations, and knew the physical layout of the plantation as well as the surrounding land. This monkey wrench had to be a regular fixture on the plantation so suspicion would not be aroused. Some manner of disguise such as a profession or menial position must have been engaged by this extremely clever and forceful entity. We also believe that the monkey wrench had access to free blacks and whites who were in positions to intervene, intercede, or provide shelter for the fugitives. When visiting the Frederick Douglass house on Cedar Hill in Washington, D.C., we were struck by the sight of a Monkey Wrench Quilt covering one of the family beds. The National Parks Service curator confirmed that the quilt belonged to the Douglass family according to the cite records, but was unable to identify the maker. Ozella interpreted the Monkey Wrench to be the most knowledgeable person on the plantation. Was Frederick Douglass, an orator, writer, and abolitionist, a free black "monkey wrench"? Douglass, similar to the many black preachers who served the slave communities, had access to a network of people extending from the cabin steps of slaves in the South to the ports of freedom in the North.

Most Underground Railroad scholars from Wilbur Siebert to Benjamin Quarles have recognized the pivotal role of the free black community in helping runaway slaves make the journey from the plantation to the free state of Ohio and beyond. Escaping slaves had to depend heavily on the free black community, as well as their fellow slaves who remained behind. In his 1997 book *Black Jacks: African American Seamen in the Age of Sail,* Professor W. Jeffrey Bolster of the University of New Hampshire logs numerous examples, disclosing names, dates, and locations of black seamen and their role in assisting slaves to flee. Was the monkey wrench a black sailor who knew how to turn the wagon or ship's wheel, to navigate by looking to the sky and following the stars?

The wagon wheel seems an obvious code name for the fugitive slave

Alice Neal Quilt Collection of Eli Leon

party, since wagons were one of the primary means of transporting runaways. Writers from former slaves to Wilbur Siebert record the numerous
stories of escape in wagons with hidden compartments. The wagon was
for many the chariot that was to carry them home. In American quilt patterns there are many wheel patterns, ranging from simple circles and

spokes to the more elaborate carpenter's wheel in which diamonds, squares, and triangles combine to form what appears to be a starlike center or wheel within a larger flame-inspired wheel (see color photo section).

We find it fascinating that the Carpenter's Wheel pattern, along with the other quilt patterns cited in the Quilt Code, appears on a famous African American quilt known as the Alice Neal Quilt (see illustration). The Carpenter's Wheel pattern would have particular relevance for members of a "craft" society. The pattern also bears religious significance in that Jesus was a carpenter, and many spirituals instruct the slave listener to "steal away" to Jesus, to "run to Jesus"; therefore, to "follow the carpenter's wheel to the west-northwest." We see the Carpenter's Wheel pattern as the visual equivalent to spirituals such as "Steal Away." We feel that the Carpenter's Wheel is comparable to Ezekiel's wheel, which ran by faith and the grace of God. We view the setting sun as a blazing wheel of fire descending behind the mountains to the west of those fugitives moving through the Appalachians toward Ohio.

The Bear's Paw quilt pattern is an early nineteenth-century pattern that migrated from one part of America to another. According to quilt historians including Ruth Finley, the Bear's Paw pattern was prominent in the Firelands, also known as the Western or Connecticut Reserve, lands reserved for settlers whose places were burned out in Connecticut and elsewhere in the East during the Revolutionary War.

The code informs us that the wagon wheel traveled on a bear's paw trail toward the crossroads. Since the crossroads is already identified as Cleveland, Ohio, may we not assume that the bear's paw trail is a trail through the mountains? The region of Ohio known as the Firelands was famous for its bear population, so much so that, according to Siebert and others, the region was rife with stories about bears. According to Fireland Publications, nowhere is this clearer than in American folklore, where pioneer stories surrounding the Bear's Paw quilt pattern are in abundance.

This pattern consists of several squares, rectangles, and right triangles. When different scraps of fabric are used, the pattern takes on the complexity of a map that is remarkably similar in design to the African Hausa embroidered map of a village (see color photo section). The Hausa embroidery and the Bear's Paw pattern share shapes and a centralized design. The pattern contains the basic shapes and arrangement that lends itself to mapping a plantation. A one-to-one comparison reveals the following:

Hausa King's House	Plantation Big House
Hausa Mosque	Plantation "Praise" House
Hausa workshops	Plantation blacksmith shop, weaving house, carpenter's shop, kitchen, etc.

Just as the Hausa design defines the perimeter of the village and identifies major landmarks, the Bear's Paw pattern could be used to identify landmarks on the border of the plantation because its composition of squares, rectangles, and triangles reflects Hausa map designs.

Frequently, quilt patterns are given regionally relevant names. Thus, in Ohio, where bears were in abundance during the early 1800s, the pattern was called Bear's Paw. In locations where bears were scarce, the Bear's Paw pattern was given other names. In Philadelphia the pattern was called Hand of Friendship by the Quaker community, and Duck's-Foot-in-the-Mud is its Long Island, New York, name (Finley, pp. 97–99).

Because the bears lived in the mountains and knew their way around, their tracks served as road maps enabling the fugitives to navigate their way through the mountains. The sun assisted by casting shadows, turning trees into compass needles and sundials. With the sun moving from east to west and the bears trails moving in many directions, the fugitive party was able to choose which bear trail they wanted in order to travel north-northwest. The bears' trails formed a map. All the "wagon wheel" needed to do was to move along a bear's paw trail to the crossroads to Cleveland, according to Ozella.

Ozella was insistent that the bear's paw trail was a real trail. If the fugitives literally followed the trail of a bear, they would find a route through the mountains. Most escapes took place during springtime, when bears were roaming through, over, and around the mountains, visiting valleys when necessary, searching for food after their long winter's nap. Streams in the mountains and rivers in the valleys provided a supply of water and fish. Rivers, streams, and woods could also have served as landmarks. Other landmarks, like unusual rock formations or oddly shaped trees, would serve as signposts marking routes.

A children's story, *Sweet Clara and the Freedom Quilt*, illustrates how fabric patches could represent natural landmarks and be incorporated into a quilt that mapped paths from one landmark to the next on a trail to freedom. *Sweet Clara*'s author, Deborah Hopkinson, tells the story of a young slave girl named Clara who serves as seamstress in the Big House. She is separated from her mother and dreams that one day they will be reunited. Knowing that will never happen unless they are both free, Clara decides to escape, planning to pick up her mother from a neighboring plantation. Realizing that a visual guide was needed, a "picture of the land," Clara resolves to sew a map in the form of a quilt so that she and other slaves could follow the patches, patterns, and stitches to freedom. Personal conversations and correspondence with Hopkinson and the book's illustrator, James Ransom, revealed that neither has any idea of where the story originated, though Ms. Hopkinson remembers hearing a true story about the Underground Railroad on the radio, on which she based the story. Ransom, himself a descendant of slaves, modeled his illustrations on his ancestral home, the Verona Plantation on the Virginia/North Carolina border, a plantation that was owned by Captain James Ransom.

Within the context of *Sweet Clara*, we find all the elements that are referenced in the Underground Railroad Quilt Code. In 1993 Ozella pointed to the stitching on one of her quilts and said, "Slaves used quilts to communicate. The length of the stitches and the position of the stitches formed a language that only the slaves would know." With amazing parallels to *Sweet Clara*, Clara uses stitches that represent roads and landmarks to herself and are also readable by the other slaves.

In 1997 Ozella demonstrated how placing quilt ties every two inches apart created a grid that was discernible on the back of the quilt. When questioned about the grid, she explained that it constituted a scale and enabled the slaves to chart locations and distances. Clara creates a grid by arranging fabric in an alternating Nine Patch/Plain Block pattern. She makes a "picture of the land" using fabric. Clara states: "Then one day I was sewin' a patch on a pretty blue blanket. The patch looked just the same shape as the cow pond near the cabins. The little stitches looked like a path going all round it. Here it was—a picture that wouldn't wash away. A map!" (Hopkinson, p. 13). The Nine Patch is an easy pattern for beginning quilters. But in *Sweet Clara*, the Nine Patch pattern forms visually identifiable fields of different crops, depending on the colors of fabric used in the pattern. In this way, the Nine Patch helps form the plantation map (see color photo section).

Clara wisely asked other slaves what they knew about the different fields and the layout of the land surrounding her plantation. She listened carefully when slaves who had traveled to different locations off the plantation described what they had seen. The plantation driver provided Clara with mileage distances to sew into her quilt. Clara then interpreted what she heard into squares and blocks of fabric and stitched it into her quilt. When other slaves saw what Clara was doing, the quilt became a communal project, with everyone wanting to contribute to it.

The cook's husband told her about a swamp and how to pass through it. Clara is sewing on the back of the quilt at the time. A quilter usually quilts with the top of the quilt facing up so that the quilting stitches are in the space determined by the piecework design. At this point, the book's illustrator shows the quilt's backing, which appears to be parallel rows of light brown lines with large pale green dots in between. Why show Clara stitching the backing? Is the illustrator, James Ransom, betraying his knowledge or remembrance of special stitches, similar to those of Mrs. Scott? And what about Clara's description of her quilt: Does it not sound like Mrs. Scott's recollection of her Plantation Quilt? Clara says, ". . . I had blue calico and flowered blue silk for creeks and rivers, and greens and blue-greens for the fields, and white sheeting for roads." Clara knew where to place her fabric fields, thanks to the cook's husband, who says, ". . . word is they gon' plant corn in the three west fields on the Verona Plantation this year." The plantation driver, another source of information, says, "I heard the master sayin' yesterday he didn't want to travel to Mr. Morse's place 'cause it's over twenty miles north o'here."

From the observations of the cook's husband and the driver we learn that Clara could enter detailed topographical information regarding the distance of a neighboring plantation and the layout of the surrounding land. It is interesting that the figure of twenty miles was used. In Siebert's Underground Railroad publication, twenty miles is often cited as the distance between "safe houses" or "stations."

In the moments following the completion of the quilt, Clara speaks to her Aunt Rachel about the final patch representing the hidden boat that would take Clara and anyone else across the Ohio River. Finally, Clara and Aunt Rachel turn their attention to the star sewn at the top of the quilt. It indicated the North Star, the star that Aunt Rachel told Clara, early on, hung above Canada. On the day that Clara and her companion, Jack, left the plantation, there was a torrential rainstorm. According to Aunt Rachel, the rains lasted three days. This kind of storm, in which there is constant rain for several days, occurs only in springtime. Summer brings storms but no lasting rains; autumn sees lasting rains but no storms. Only in the springtime are the two combined, as in the story of Sweet Clara. Ozella stated that slaves would leave in the springtime. This would be the optimum time to make the long, perilous journey north.

When Sweet Clara escaped, she left her quilt behind so that others might study it and follow, because she herself had been able to memorize the quilt-map. On the road to freedom, Clara recognized landmarks and knew which way to turn. The story thus makes direct reference to the African use of mnemonic devices. Clara associated places, streams, rivers, and numerous landmarks with the fabric and designs she stitched. Seeing her quilt every day as she worked on it enabled her to memorize the individual patterns, their meanings, and the configuration of the whole quilt. The quilt then becomes the everyday object, encoded with a secret message that could only be read by those trained to "read" the symbols. As a mnemonic device, the quilt triggers memory.

We have considered how a knowledgeable but mysterious person or

persons guided the fugitives from the plantation to the Appalachian mountain range, where they followed the trail of a bear until they crossed over into Ohio on the way to Cleveland, the crossroads. Once they arrived at the crossroads, their lives changed permanently.

Monkey Wrench Quilt as Displayed in the Frederick Douglass House in Washington, D.C. (#FRD02171) Courtesy of the National Park Service, Frederick Douglass National Historic Site

"Once they got to the crossroads they dug a log cabin on the ground. Shoofly told them to dress up in cotton and satin bow ties and go to the cathedral church, get married, and exchange double wedding rings."

Chapter Five

"Once They Got to the Crossroads..."

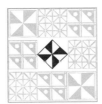

THAT THE CROSSROADS MENTIONED IN THE CODE REFERRED TO Cleveland, Ohio, seems correct. Most scholars, led by the seminal nineteenth-century publications of Wilbur Siebert, and the recent National Park Service work on the Underground Railroad document Cleveland as a major terminal. Abolitionist Alexander Ross constantly cites Cleveland as a meeting place or point of departure. His code poetically describes the city of Cleveland as Hope, an appropriate description for a city sitting at the crossroads of many paths to freedom. Four or five overland trails connected with numerous water routes crossing Lake Erie into Canada.

West African cultures manifest the concept of the crossroads as well. Robert Farris Thompson notes that the Yoruba god Eshu is the embodiment of the crossroads. Often represented in sculptural form,

The Crossroads Pattern

Eshu can be seen wearing a cap with one side red and the other side black, representing, as the messenger god, the eternal lesson of arriving at the crossroads, "knowing what is truth and what is falsehood, or else the lessons of the crossroads—the point where doors open or close, where persons have to make decisions that may forever after affect their lives—will be lost" (Thompson, p. 19) (see illustration).

Symbolically the Kongo crossroads is represented by a cross, made in the shape of what we know as a Greek cross, with vertical and horizontal intersecting lines of equal length. This cross, according to Kongo scholar

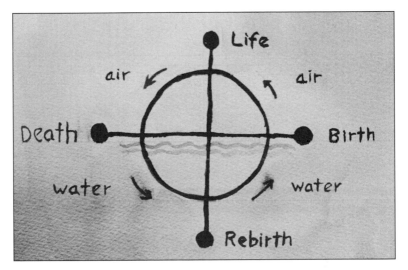

Kongo Cosmogram Modeled After Thompson

Wyatt MacGaffey, is often marked on the ground to indicate the point where a person taking an oath would stand. In Kongo symbology, this person is standing at the intersection between the Ancestors and the living, the horizontal line being the division between the two (Thompson, p. 109) (see illustration). What would be a more accurate representation of arrival in Cleveland, the axis of many roads leading to freedom, than the concept of the African crossroad, the point at which a final decision affecting the rest of one's life must be made?

Though Ozella thought there might have been an actual log cabin just outside of Cleveland, the crossroads, none of our research uncovered any such cabin. She also said that the code might be directing the slaves to actually build a log cabin, perhaps to weather out winter or establish permanent residency in a "free" area. By this she thought that a certain amount of time was being spoken about—the time it might take to actually construct a log cabin.

Of course, with population growth and urban renewal, it is hardly likely that we would find a log cabin dating back to the early 1800s still intact unless it was being preserved by a historical society. In any event, Ozella's analysis did not satisfy our curiosity. No one would *dig* a log cabin. A log cabin would be *built*. What was the code alluding to?

For answers to this question, we turned once again to the pattern itself, Log Cabin. The Log Cabin pattern has long been associated with Underground Railroad oral history. This pattern is said to date back to colonial times, although there is some controversy among quilt scholars regarding the exact date when the centuries-old design first appeared in quilts. We do have documented examples that date at least to the 1830s, some thirty to forty years earlier than the majority of extant examples. In the South, an arrangement of roughly hewn logs or planks often formed dwellings for slaves. These "rustic" houses predate the more polished designs of the Midwest, which were romanticized during the presidency of Abraham Lincoln. Slave narratives are replete with descriptions of log or plank cabins having dirt flooring. Some of these "log cabin" slave quarters can still be seen on Southern plantations today and are largely representative of the style of shelter afforded slaves.

The Log Cabin pattern, which has alternating light and dark fabric logs arranged around a central square, bears names associated with farming. Examples of these patterns are Barn Raising, Straight Furrows, and Streak of Lightning. The Streak of Lightning arrangement is a zigzag pattern. Siebert described the positioning of safe houses in Ohio as appearing in a zigzag formation. We believe this has something to do with the African belief that evil travels along straight lines. Furthermore, for safety reasons, it would be imperative for the fugitives to travel an indirect route. Undoubtedly, traveling in zigzag fashion would have prevented slave catchers from being able to discern a predictable path of escape. (This

zigzag manner of travel shows up more directly when we discuss the
Drunkard's Path pattern in the next chapter.)

Researchers like Gladys-Marie Fry have combed through many slave
narratives looking for clues to the meaning of quilt patterns used by
slaves. In her book *Stitched from the Soul: Slave Quilts from the Ante-Bellum
South*, Dr. Fry lists quilt pattern names that were favored by slave quilters.
The list, gleaned from slave narrative documents and inventories, identi-
fies the Log Cabin pattern along with such patterns as Birds All Over the
Elements, Little Boy's Breeches, Drunkard's Path, Railroad Crossing,
Tree of Paradise, Double Star, Feathered Star, Cotton Leaf, and Nine
Patch (Fry, pp. 45–46).

It was Fry who *first* suggested that a Log Cabin quilt with a black center was a signal on the Underground Railroad. The usual color of the center square of Log Cabin quilts of this era was red, because the center
square was supposed to represent the fireplace, the hearth in the cabin.
Critics of Fry's theory were quick to point out that black fabric was not
commercially produced until the last decades of the nineteenth century.
However, narratives and other nineteenth-century records show that
slaves and others were able to make the black fabric color through an or-
ganic dying process. Black fabric was available but scarce and rarely seen
until the Victorian era made it a popular color.

In an article published in 1994, Raymond Dobard proposed that the
center of the Log Cabin quilt was probably a dark indigo blue, given that
slaves brought with them to America a tradition of making indigo dye. In
fact, a recently published article tells how indigo-dyed cloth is fashioned
into clothing known as "Black Clothes," which southern Senegalese Jola
men wear upon emerging from the sacred forest at the end of an initiation
ritual. Although the indigo garments range from medium to dark blue, all
are considered "Black Clothes." For the Jola, and conceivably for members of the Underground Railroad, indigo blue cloth was referred to as

"black" (see Peter Mark, Ferdinand De Jong, and Clemence Chupin, "Ritual and Masking Traditions in Jola Men's Initiation," *African Arts,* Winter 1998, pp. 36–47).

Quilt researcher Sandi Fox, in an article about Log Cabin quilts and the migration westward, interprets the midcentury quilts with yellow centers as representing the "function of the cabin as a light or beacon in the wilderness" (Fox, pp. 6–10). Is it possible that the yellow centers on Log Cabin quilts of this era also signaled a safe house?

We believe that William Lloyd Still, the famous black Underground Railroad conductor, was also familiar with the Log Cabin pattern. His account of the Underground Railroad, gleaned from interviews with hundreds of slaves he assisted to freedom, is also personally associated with the Log Cabin quilt pattern. The Still family quilt is a Log Cabin quilt with a yellow center. The Still family resided in Philadelphia. Since most log cabins were found in the Midwest, why would the Stills choose as their family quilt the symbol of the log cabin if there wasn't a connection between the Log Cabin pattern and the Underground Railroad? And is it just a coincidence that the Still family quilt would have a yellow center? Perhaps it was used to signal that their home was a safe house, as oral history has intimated. In Africa, the color yellow is used to signify life. Could this color symbolism have meaning here as well?

Raymond adds to the questions concerning color signaling in "A Covenant in Cloth: the Visible and Tangible in African American Quilts," an article on quilts in Illinois life in which he considers the yellow center of Log Cabin quilts. A yellow-centered Log Cabin quilt, Raymond suggests, may signal the fugitive slave to take leave.

Because few Log Cabin quilts have survived any period prior to the 1870s does not automatically mean that they were not made before 1870. The Log Cabin quilt, with its raised "log" surface and tied rather than quilted center, is more vulnerable to wear and tear. Consider, too, the fact that the Log Cabin quilt was a rustic bedcover rather than a fancy display quilt. As such, it was exposed to greater use. Is it any wonder, then, that like the rustic slave dwellings of the same name, most early (pre-1870) Log Cabin quilts did not survive? Remarkably, one example did surface in our investigation. The Raleigh Township Centennial Museum in North Buxton, Canada, houses a Log Cabin quilt, which, according to museum curator Alice Newby, was made by fugitive slaves who had successfully made the journey from slavery to freedom and reached the black fugitive community of Buxton. This would be proof that, indeed, the Log Cabin quilt pattern did exist prior to the Civil War.

As we have noted, "dug a log cabin" is unusual phrasing, as is "on the ground." Do these phrases refer to the actual building of a log cabin, as suggested by Ozella, or to something else? After watching the film *Daughters of the Dust*, by Julie Dash, we felt we had an answer. In this film the male characters are shown meeting each other on a dirt road and, with no verbal exchange, inscribing something in the dirt between them. Something is obviously being communicated. This clue suggested that once again we look to African traditions. Robert Farris Thompson in *Flash of the Spirit* discusses the ritual of the Ejagham, who would inscribe symbols from their writing system, *nsibidi*, on the ground, to invoke spirits, both good and bad. Thompson states that both the Fon and Kongo practice the tradition of creating ritual ground designs, sometimes to control a crisis situation or even to honor the funeral of a very important person (Thompson, p. 228).

In a personal interview with Prince Hall historian Joseph Walkes, Jr., he stated that it was traditional for both black and white Masons to identify each other by drawing a Masonic symbol on the ground. This technique would be used to show recognition when the Masons were in an area where it would be unsafe to verbalize their "brotherhood."

It is our conjecture that "dug a cabin on the ground" refers to the act of drawing a symbol on the ground in order to recognize persons with whom it was safe to communicate. We suggest that at least some of these persons were Prince Hall Masons, familiar with symbols of African as well as American derivation. Who better to secretly aid the fugitives than free blacks in a secret society of their own? With both African and American parallels, this act would be familiar to those with secrets to keep. Once again we see used a technique that allows for communication when it is unsafe to communicate with voice or words.

Who or what was Shoofly? What did it mean to dress up in cotton and satin bow ties? Did the cathedral church refer to an actual church, and if so, why the redundancy in phrasing? A cathedral is a church. Why not say go to the church or go to the cathedral? What did getting married mean? Who was marrying whom? What sort of union or contract was involved? To exchange double wedding rings was more than an anomaly for the fugitives, who were more accustomed to jumping the broom than bestowing even a single wedding band as a sign of their union.

In previous parts of the code, the names of quilt patterns helped us understand a symbolic meaning, and although Shoofly, Bow Tie or Tie, and possibly Cathedral Church were quilt patterns familiar to nineteenth-century quilters, the Double Wedding Ring pattern did not exist until the end of the century. Thus, this quilt name would not be familiar to seamstresses of any color. Upon first hearing the code, we had asked ourselves whether all the quilt patterns mentioned were popular and familiar to both black and white seamstresses prior to the Civil War. Cuesta Benberry was the first to point out to us that the Double Wedding Ring was not a pre–Civil War quilt pattern.

Ozella thought that Shoofly referred to an actual person who might have aided escaping slaves, but she had no further information. Was Shoofly representative of free blacks who may have been secretly aiding and harboring fugitives? Many times in the discussion of the code, Ozella stated that it was the "mathematicians" who devised the code in the first place and that these mathematicians were similar to what we know of today as fraternities. Was this a reference, once again, to the Masons? We knew that the first African American Masonic Lodge was established by Prince Hall prior to the Revolutionary War in Boston. Signs and symbols are a very important part of the "secret" symbolic language of the Masons. We also knew that as early as 1801, a white Masonic Lodge was established in Charleston, South Carolina. Since members of this lodge would most certainly have included plantation owners, it is not hard to believe, as Joseph Walkes, Jr., has suggested, that house slaves could have observed Masonic rituals enacted by their masters. Nor is it too far-fetched to believe that free blacks from the North, some of them members of the Prince Hall Masons, would have traveled to South Carolina prior to the Civil War to conduct business. These facts and conjectures have led to our belief that the mathematicians could have been members of Masonic organizations. Since the structure and language of Masonic orders are mathematics, specifically geometry, and refer to the building of King Solomon's temple, what better way to devise a code than by creating a symbolic language based on geometric patterns of similar design to Masonic symbols? Perhaps Shoofly, who seems to be directing the action in this part of the code, was a Prince Hall Mason or a free black familiar with a secret language.

Ozella told us that dressing up in cotton and satin bow ties was a direction to the slaves to dress in a formal manner. She stated that she thought there was an actual church where slaves would go and be aided in taking off their chains, as represented by the double wedding rings, but she could not state where such a church might be located. She noted that the stained-glass windows often found in churches would afford cover so that no one might look inside the church and discover the fugitives. In further discussions of these words, Ozella suggested that exchanging double wedding rings might also symbolize letting go the bonds of slavery.

Caves and caverns are found throughout the Blue Ridge and Allegheny mountain ranges, parts of the Appalachians. Slaves traveling these mountains might have discovered such caves to hide in. Mark Twain's references to caves in Tom Sawyer and Huckleberry Finn provide another clue. Twain designates several caves as looking like "cathedrals." Mammoth Cave in Kentucky and Carlsbad Caverns in New Mexico both have rooms labeled "cathedral" because of the majestic stalactites and stalagmites decorating vast chambers, making them look and feel like the great cathedrals of Europe. Might not the cathedral mentioned in this code refer to a specific cave or cavern the fugitives could find respite in? Many escapees and outlaws have used caves as hiding places; might not the fleeing fugitives hide in caves as well?

History has documented that graveyards were frequently the hiding place for fugitive slaves, often because of their proximity to rivers and their locations on the outskirts of town. Sometimes these graveyards were located near churches. Often there were chapels and large family mausoleums in graveyards near major cities. Was the cathedral church one of these? Might the cathedral church reference a particular graveyard church?

To dress up in cotton and satin bow ties is a bit easier to decipher. Escaping slaves were clothed in the most distinguishable of garments. Obviously their clothing would get worn and tattered and give away their status as runaways. Levi Coffin writes about how free blacks would often meet the slaves and give them fresh clothing. Once clothes were exchanged, members of the fugitive party could accompany the free black citizens back to their houses. It was easier to hide fugitive slaves with people of their own color. They would not stand out, especially if dressed in similar fashion. Might not cotton and satin bow ties, therefore, be a reference not only to changing one's clothes but also to disguising oneself? Might not this phrase also be a direction to dress up in order not to stand out among city folks if, in one of the final legs of their journey, the fugitives were to walk through town to get to the ships awaiting them? Sunbonnets were one means of disguise.

In the nineteenth century, sunbonnets and bandannas were indicators of social rank for women. Bonnets were worn by women above the rank of slave and indentured servants and would help fleeing slaves disguise themselves by obscuring their faces. Social custom at that time dictated that a woman tilt her head slightly down, with her eyes looking shyly to the ground. We know that Harriet Tubman made use of the bonnet as a means of disguise.

Around John Brown's Cave, a local Underground Railroad site in Nebraska City, Nebraska, stories still circulate about a minister who used to drive his wagon with two sunbonneted ladies sitting beside him. A half hour later, the minister would return with two ladies still sitting beside him. What no one seemed to notice was that on this return trip, the two women wearing the bonnets had dark complexions. Sunbonnets were also the disguise used to transport fugitives to the banks of the Missouri River so they could cross from Nebraska City to Tabor, Iowa.

From a quilter's perspective we are led to other connections. The Bow Tie quilt patterns have been popular in America for nearly two centuries. The simplest of these patterns consist of only four equilateral triangles that form a square. To visualize the Bow Tie pattern, picture an X placed in a square so that it touches all four corners. Darken the triangles on the sides, and a stylized Bow Tie appears. Turn the design on its side and an Hourglass pattern is created. Arranged in this fashion, this pattern would be very familiar to African secret society members, especially the Poro, who saw it representing protection. The Bow Tie pattern is also similar to the Kongo cosmogram with its "four moments of the sun" (see Ozella's Underground Railroad Quilt Code patterns, pp. 189–193). The triangular quadrants indicate morning, midday, evening, and night. The Bow Tie quilt pattern thus has the potential of forming a compass and a sundial in cloth (see illustration). The same Bow Tie pattern is known as well to Masonic members here in America. For the Masons, the hourglass was a symbol of time well managed, a virtue the society held highly. One was to make the best use of time (see illustration p. 194).

Secondary patterns might also be created from the Bow Tie pattern that are of special significance to the African American community. Changing the arrangement of the triangles creates patterns known as Pinwheel and Broken Dishes. Broken dishes arranged on a grave site remains to this day a superstition among Southern African Americans. The concept of the Pinwheel may refer to the Kongo cosmogram, a superstition, or a way to determine which way the wind is blowing. All these patterns stem from the basic Bow Tie quilt pattern.

We know that Africans arriving in the South Carolina area came from cultures wherein secret society membership was a rite of passage. Secret society members would be acquainted with various symbols that held special meaning to them. One of those symbols, found in the secret societies of the Aiyasa, Oro, Epe, Mborko, and Sindungo, is the geometric pattern known to us as the hourglass shape, or, as seen above, known in American quilting as the Bow Tie patterns when positioned horizontally. Of even more interest was the discovery that this same symbol was used in the Masonic order, both white and black. Thus, both African secret societies as well as Masons in America share a symbol, the geometric hourglass figure. Might the Bow Tie pattern be a reference to a familiar "secret" symbol? One that might imply to escaping slaves, that they were among friends? Would free blacks, under the guise of their membership in the Prince Hall Masonic Order, use the familiar Masonic/ African symbol of the hourglass (Bow Tie quilt pattern) to signal escaping slaves that they could be trusted? Could this particular geometric design be one inscribed on the ground to indicate common allegiances?

Thus, this phrase in the code might be understood in terms of using a disguise, hiding in caves or caverns and/or identifying helpful people through the use of familiar symbols.

We were left to ponder the mystery of the Double Wedding Ring reference. While Ozella referred to the Double Wedding Ring as symbolizing getting rid of the chains the slaves might still be wearing, she also stated that it was essential for the slaves to also rid themselves of the mental bonds of slavery. If we look at the Double Wedding Ring concept in the context of the whole phrase, we are left with the idea that double wedding rings was not referencing the later well-known twentieth-century quilt pattern of the same name but rather referencing either actual chains of bondage worn by the slaves or mental chains of bondage. In either case, the slaves would be required to rid themselves of the chains and undergo a transformation, both physical as well as mental: from slave to free. In a later conversation, Ozella further explained that there were two quilt patterns identifying chains: the Double Wedding Ring and the Double Irish Chain. Both are popular quilt patterns but of differing dates. The Irish Chain is a well-known nineteenth-century pattern, while the Double Wedding Ring is a twentieth-century creation. Both visually could be read as stylized chains. The Double Wedding Ring remains an unsolved mystery for us. It makes sense in the code if we do not make it a quilt pattern name. We suspect that this is a case where the Double Wedding Ring reference was not a quilt pattern name. It probably meant something else. Perhaps the "double wedding ring" was referencing an audible signal, the ringing of a bell, two times?

We agree with Ozella that one of the most important tasks facing any escaping slaves would be freeing themselves of the mental chains of slavery, whether implied by the Double Wedding Rings or not. The journey to freedom would require not just the change in geography; it would require a change in perspective of oneself from enslaved to free.

"Flying geese stay on the drunkard's path
and follow the stars."

Chapter Six

"Flying Geese Stay on the Drunkard's Path . . ."

OZELLA ASKED, "WHAT DIRECTION DO THE GEESE FLY?" SHE THEN answered her own question by saying, "Geese fly north in the spring-time or summer." Ozella interpreted the Flying Geese pattern as a di-rection as well as an indication of the best season for slaves to escape. She said that the flying geese pointed to the direction, north, for the slaves to move. She also mentioned that geese would have to stop at wa-terways along their journey in order to rest and eat. According to Ozella, slaves were to take their cues on direction, timing, and behav-ior from the migrating geese.

This part of the code was easy for us to decipher because of the obvious symbolism. The flying geese were the fleeing slaves. We found that the image of flying geese was inspiration for several quilt patterns. One that dates back at least to the beginning of the nineteenth century is an arrangement of equilateral triangles in which the triangles appear to follow each other. Like most quilt patterns, this particular pattern is known by several names. It was published in the *Ohio Farmer* in 1894 as Wheel and in 1898 as Dutchman's Wheel. The same pattern is also called Wild Goose Chase and Dutchman's Puzzle (Brackman, *Encyclopedia of Pieced Quilt Patterns*, p. 178). The formation points to four directions, with two triangles pointing north, two pointing west, two pointing south and two pointing east in a counter-clockwise movement (see color photo section). A clever quilter would be able to specify one direction by the use of fabric pieces. For example, if a quilter wanted to indicate a northern direction, she/he would simply make one set of triangles distinct from the others (see color photo section). What sets the one set of triangles apart from the others is the unique, yet subtle use of fabric. If all sets of triangles are sewn in a two fabric combination, and only one set has a third fabric, that set will be different from the others to the discerning eye. The fabric choice makes this possible.

A clear example of distinguishing one set from the others can be seen in the Deborah Coates quilt as pictured in the book *Hearts and Hands*. The pattern displayed on this quilt was not identified in the seminal publication of *Hearts and Hands,* but was subsequently identified by Raymond in his 1994 article "Quilts as Communal Emblems and Personal Icons" (Dobard, p. 39). In this article, Raymond writes that the pattern is well known as Birds in the Air. He goes on to link the pattern to the Gladys-Marie Fry listing of patterns that slaves preferred. Fry calls the pattern Birds All Over the Elements. Barbara Brackman writes that the pattern was also named Flying Birds, Flight of Swallows, and Flock of Geese. There appears to be a link between the Coates quilt pattern and the concept of flight. Was this pattern a coded reference to the flight of the fugitives? We know that the Coates house was Station #5 on the Underground Railroad (Dobard, p. 39). If one looks closely at the Coates

quilt, one can see that there is a section in the pattern distinctly different from the rest of the quilt. While the triangles point down in the majority of the quilt, in one small section in the middle of the quilt on the
right-hand side, a group of triangles point northward. Is this merely by
chance? We believe Deborah Coates intended the triangles to be a visual nod to the Underground Railroad. The only reason we know the
significance of this quilt is family oral history that has finally been written down.

Deborah Coates was the wife of prominent Quaker abolitionist
Lindley Coates, who was among the organizers of the Anti-Slavery
Society and who preceded William Lloyd Garrison as president of
American Anti-Slavery Association in 1840. Lindley and Deborah
Coates's home in Sadsbury, Lancaster County, Pennsylvania, was Station
#5 on one route of the Underground Railroad.

Both Birds in the Air and Flying Geese belong to a family of quilt patterns in which flight is the theme. Migrating birds or geese instinctively
knew in which direction to fly. For the fugitives, quilt patterns provided directions. The flexibility that this Flying Geese pattern offers would enable
a quilter to use it as a compass on a sampler quilt or any quilt where many
patterns are placed together. The sampler quilt, a quilt exhibiting a "sam-
ple," one each of many quilt patterns, was the perfect quilt type in which
to hide many patterns and their meaning in plain view. The position of one
or more directional patterns, and the inclusion of patterns identifying
landmarks could transform a quilt into a map. Once a direction was established, the fugitives were able to travel on. They were to do so as if they
were following a drunkard's path.

Following a drunkard's path is a clear warning, as Ozella suggested,
for the slaves to move in a staggering fashion so as to allude any following
slave hunters. While following a drunkard's path out of Charleston may
lead to several possible routes, there is one route that lends itself to his-

torical documentation. A crooked line from Charleston northward between the Piedmont and the mountains of the Carolinas and Virginia
brings the fugitives to Wheeling, Virginia (located in the state of West
Virginia today). The area near Wheeling is documented by Siebert as one
of the major crossing places for slaves escaping from Virginia through the
mountains. A local citizen and historian of Dresden, Ohio, provided us
with much information about his beloved town nestled in the foothills of
the Appalachians. Dresden is situated to the west of Wheeling and the
south of Cleveland, in Coshocton County. Coshocton County is noted in
several published abolitionists' memoirs, but is most highlighted in
Wilbur Siebert's work. The "drunkard's path" could very well have
zigzagged from the plantations near Charleston up through Coshocton
County. The fugitives stayed on this drunkard's path and followed the
stars.

When we asked Ozella about the drunkard's path, she turned a quilt
over and focused on the reverse side. Running her fingers along the
threads, she said, "Drunkards weave back and forth, never moving in a
straight line." She believed the Drunkard's Path pattern was a warning to
slaves to move in zigzag fashion and to even double back occasionally on
their tracks in order to elude any slave catchers who were pursuing them.

Ozella did not elaborate on the phrase "follow the stars." She had
spoken earlier about the importance, however, of the North Star as a
guiding light for fleeing slaves. Like the star of Bethlehem guiding the
Wise Men, the North Star has been historically connected with the
Underground Railroad. We see references to it in Frederick Douglass's
newspaper, *The North Star*; in spirituals; in the folk song "Follow the
Drinking Gourd"; and in the words of Underground Railroad conductor
Harriet Tubman when she instructed her "passengers" to "follow the
North Star." Down through the ages, the North Star has always been
critical to navigation on the seas as well as land travel, so it is not surpris-

ing to see "follow the stars" in the Underground Railroad Quilt Code. We found, however, that the phrase did not specifically state the North Star. As it was meant to be a code, perhaps a reference to the North Star would have been too obvious. But another possible reason came to light.

During a visit to the Smithsonian Institution we were struck by a Native American exhibit on "star maps." On display was a replica of a star map, used in a sacred ceremony of the Pawnee, that was clearly a map of the heavens at a particular time of year. Made out of buckskin, the original star map is a part of the permanent collection at the Field Museum in Chicago. Crosses and dots are used to symbolize various constellations. Several museum curators, skilled in Native American studies, confirmed that star maps were commonly used by Native Americans during the nineteenth century. While "Americans" mapped the land, the Native Americans mapped the heavens. Moreover, some African peoples, most notably the Dogon of Mali, whose astronomical accuracy still baffles scholars, mapped the stars. History tells us that many escaped slaves eventually settled with Native populations and that the cultures and traditions of the Africans and Natives often overlapped. It would not be so surprising to find that the Native and African traditions of looking to the heavens might have been used by escaping slaves. Might not the Underground Railroad Quilt Code reference to "follow the stars" mean to follow certain constellations or specific stars taught to escaping slaves? While we can only surmise which constellations might have aided escape, the historical precedent for using the stars as guiding lights has been firmly established.

The "drinking gourd," or Big Dipper, always points to the North Star, in the handle of the Little Dipper. In many African American quilts, the North Star is represented in the guise of the evening star. This eight-pointed star is one that oral history and folklore honor as a guiding light for fugitive slaves. Whether the North Star is called the drinking gourd or known as the pattern the Evening Star, it was like the star of Bethlehem for the fugitives seeking freedom. Imagine the connections slaves would make when forced to attend a Christian Christmas service that might include the recitation of the story of Mary and Jesus and the three Wise Men following the star of Bethlehem to find the location of the Christ child, the savior of the world. Imagine them later hearing that their own freedom could be had if they only followed the North Star to Canada and freedom. *Most* slave owners were not aware of the symbolic imagery they were teaching their slaves by forcing them to attend Christian church service.

Since the beginning of time, the North Star has been important to navigation. Sailors, including black sailors, needed the stars in order to sail to their destination. It is interesting that the Underground Railroad Quilt Code ends with a reference to the stars when the fugitives are at the crossroads—Cleveland. Perhaps this phrase could be understood in another fashion. Might the statement that the fugitives followed the stars allude to voyage by sea and the possible assistance of black sailors and/or black sea captains such as William Wells Brown, who, after seizing his freedom, worked for nine years as a steamboatman on Lake Erie.

Usually thoughts about the Underground Railroad involve images of dangerous, secretive travel over land. Seldom does the thought of sea ports, ships, and smuggling fugitives out of bondage automatically come to mind. However, the Underground Railroad incorporated numerous lines by sea, lake, river, and canal. Once again we are fascinated by Siebert's *The Underground Railroad*, a book filled with stories about sailing to freedom on Lake Erie. Siebert logs captains, vessels, and the cities of Cleveland, Sandusky, and Detroit in his work. One poignant story involves a Captain Shepard and his boat named *Walk-in-the-Water*.

Captain Shepard ran a boat from Sandusky, Ohio, to Detroit, Michigan. The captain was once approached by a slave owner needing assistance to find his "chattel." Captain Shepard was offered the sum of three hundred dollars for his efforts. The good captain helped the owner to diligently search for three days, but in vain. The captain even ventured a voyage from Sandusky to Detroit and back. The fugitive slave was not to be found. As soon as the frustrated owner left, Captain Shepard ferried the hidden slave from Sandusky to Fort Malden, Canada. The irony of the situation is highlighted by the wit and wisdom Captain Shepard revealed in naming his boat *Walk-in-the-Water*. The reference to the spiritual "Wade in the Water" would have been understood only by those familiar with the Underground Railroad's coded use of spirituals. The boat's name also connotes determination and the miracle of Jesus' walk on water. Surprisingly, Siebert did not make the connection (Siebert, p. 82).

Other captains and sailors whom Siebert cites include General Reed, who was a true seafaring conductor on the Underground Railroad. His fleet of boats, operating from Racine, Wisconsin, did not charge fares to fleeing fugitives. Reed's boats were the *Sultana*, under Captain Appleby, the *Madison*, the *Missouri*, the *Niagara*, and the *Keystone State*. Other mariners who contributed to the freedom cause were Captain Steele of the propeller *Galena* and Captain Kelsey of the *Chesapeake*. Proof of the Racine operation is contained in a letter of April 7, 1896, addressed to Wilbur Siebert and written by A. P. Dutton. In the correspondence, Dutton outlined his twenty years' work as an abolitionist. He knew which boats and captains were sympathetic to the plight of the fugitives. As such, Dutton was an important coordinator (Siebert, pp. 82–83).

Though informative, the Dutton letter did not provide all. Siebert went on to discover what specialized boat service existed between Chicago and Detroit. An example is Captain Blake of the *Illinois*. According to the *Firelands Pioneer* publication of July 1888, several boats ran primarily between Sandusky and Detroit. They were the *Arrow*, the *United States*, and the *Mayflower*. Siebert's ongoing communication with freedmen living in Canada supplied him with the names of boats serving Cleveland and

Detroit. The *Forest Queen,* the *Morning Star,* and the *May Queen* are listed. The *Phoebus,* a small boating service, existed between Toledo and Detroit (ibid.).

Probably the most telling story recorded in Siebert's work is the account of William Brown, a former slave who influenced a fleet of boats and wrote his autobiography, which was published in 1848. His book is entitled *Narrative of William Brown.* Siebert learned that Brown was well known in Cleveland as a friend of runaways who would carry any escaping slave to Canada on his boat, free of charge. Brown's line stopped at Cleveland, Buffalo, and Detroit. Brown once stated, "In the year 1842, I conveyed, from the first of May to the first of December, sixty-nine fugitives over Lake Erie to Canada" (Siebert, p. 83). With the help of seamen like William Wells Brown, the fugitives were able to follow the stars.

Mrs. Elizabeth Scott's 1980 Plantation Quilt offers a modern-day example of the ways stars are used in contemporary African American quilts. She has sewn a constellation of stars using appliqué, embroidery, and beading techniques. The stars represent her childhood memories of the former cotton plantation where she lived with her sharecropper parents and where her grandparents had once labored as slaves. Born in 1917, Elizabeth picked cotton as a child. In the evening, she recalls sitting on the porch, looking up at the stars, being mesmerized by the night sky. In her own words, she explains:

> This quilt calls up for me memories of the slave and farm women on the plantation who worked so hard. At six o'clock in the morning they'd be out in the fields. After they worked so hard all day, they'd work hard at night too. That's when they'd sew and make the quilts. By night they sat out on that porch and talked and pieced and sang. I recall that often the moon and stars would be so bright it would be like daylight out there.

The stars on the quilt look the way you'd see them on some of those clear nights. In the center of the quilt there's a special star. I call it a shootin' star. My parents used to call it a devil star. Every ten years this star would come through, but you couldn't see it with your naked eye. You had to look through wax cloth to see it.

These stars back home were very precious to me. They gave us so much light. They lit our way at night. They lighted up the porch. They even seemed to give off heat and warm us. (Grudin, p. 32)

The stars that Mrs. Scott remembers from her childhood were most likely those belonging to the Ursa Major constellation, better known as the Great Bear, which includes the Big Dipper. To paraphrase the words of a spiritual, "Behold That Star," the North Star was "a star up yonder," "a star to behold." The North Star was also a subject of the folk song "Follow the Drinking Gourd," in which directive is given to follow the points of the drinking gourd—the Big Dipper—to the brightest star, the North Star.

Perhaps no song is more connected to the Underground Railroad than "Follow the Drinking Gourd." This song, mainly due to its direct symbology, contains the elements of secrecy, encoded directions, and allusions that have already been mentioned. While the song has become part of the folklore in the African American tradition, the stories surrounding the discovery of the song itself warrant scrutiny for what they tell us about secrecy and the African American oral tradition.

Folklorist H. B. Parks tells the following story about the first time he heard "Follow the Drinking Gourd":

"I was a resident of Hot Springs, North Carolina, during the year 1912 and had charge of the agricultural work of a large industrial school. This school owned a considerable herd of cattle, which were kept in the meadows on the tops of the Big Rich Mountains on the boundary between

North Carolina and Tennessee. One day while riding through the mountains looking after this stock, I heard the following stanza sung by a little Negro boy, who was picking up dry sticks of wood near a Negro cabin:

Foller the drinkin' gou'd,
Foller the drinkin' gou'd;
No one know, the wise man say,
"Foller the drinkin' gou'd."

It is very doubtful if this part of the song would have attracted anyone's attention had not the old grandfather, who had been sitting on a block of wood in front of the cabin, slowly got up and, taking his cane, given the boy a sound lick across the back with the admonition not to sing that song again. This excited my curiosity and I asked the old man why he did not want the boy to sing the song. The only answer I could get was that it was bad luck." (Dobie, p. 84)

One year later Parks *heard* the song again, this time sung by a black fisherman in Louisville, Kentucky. When asked *what the song meant*, the fisherman replied that he *didn't know*. Because Parks was a white stranger, he received this response. Please realize that a white stranger in a Southern city during the heyday of Jim Crow laws was not to be trusted. Silence was a shield protecting the black community.

In 1918, Parks heard the same song once again, only with different words.

Foller the Risen Lawd,
Foller the Risen Lawd;
The bes' thing the Wise Man say,
"Foller the Risen Lawd."

The two black sixteen-year-old boys who were singing the song told Parks
that they had learned it from some revivalist preachers.

Eventually Parks was able to find out the history of the song and its
meaning. An older gentleman in College Station, Texas, supplied Parks
with four verses of the original song.

> When the sun come back,
> When the firs' quail call,
> Then the time is come
> Foller the drinkin' gou'd.

> *Chorus:*
> Foller the drinkin' gou'd,
> Foller the drinkin' gou'd;
> For the ole man say,
> "Foller the drinkin' gou'd."

> The riva's bank am a very good road,
> The dead trees show the way,
> Lef' foot, peg foot goin' on,
> Foller the drinkin' gou'd.

> The riva ends a-tween two hills,
> Foller the drinkin' gou'd;
> 'Nuther riva on the other side
> Follers the drinkin' gou'd.

> Wha the little riva
> Meet the grea' big un,
> the ole man waits—
> Foller the drinkin' gou'd.

Parks writes that he took the song and showed it to his great-uncle, who, according to family stories, had been connected with the Underground Railroad. This great-uncle of Parks's remembered that in the records of the Anti-Slavery Society there was a story of a peg-legged sailor, known as Peg Leg Joe, who made several trips to the South and taught the slaves he met a trail to follow to freedom in Canada.

As the story goes, this one-legged sailor would travel throughout the South, taking odd jobs on various plantations. While working, he would make friends with the slaves and would teach them a song, "Follow the Drinking Gourd." The following spring, many young men on the plantations that Peg Leg Joe had visited would disappear. It was believed that these young men had followed the trail left by the sailor.

Parks's great-uncle said that around 1859, Peg Leg's activities centered around the area north of Mobile, Alabama, the trail following northward to the headwaters of the Tombigbee River, through the divide, and down the Tennessee River to the Ohio River (Dobie, p. 84). The trail would be marked by the outline of a human left foot and a round spot in place of the right foot.

The hidden map within the song has been traced. Dobie is one of several writers who published the song's meaning. The drinking gourd is the Big Dipper, the ole man is Peg Leg Joe himself, and the grea' big un is the Ohio River, where the fugitive slaves would be met by Peg Leg Joe, who would take them the rest of the way to Canada.

While this story has made its way into several books, including children's books, no one but Parks has ever mentioned that there might be more than the four traditionally known stanzas to the song. Parks says that he couldn't remember the other verses. Chances are he never knew them, because in his own words he admits, "The old Negro quoted a number [of verses], which either by fault of memory or secret meaning are unintelligible and are omitted" (Dobie, p. 84). What secrets might the missing verses reveal to us?

What is perhaps even more remarkable about Parks and his first encounter with the song is the reaction of the black grandfather to a white man overhearing the song. We believe that the grandfather, by reprimanding his grandchild, was instilling in him the importance of keeping the song a secret. Even in 1928, more than half a century after the Emancipation, this story points to the value of secrecy in some African American families.

The fact that a degree of secrecy seems to permeate some segments of the African American culture was also noted when Raymond was invited to attend the McFaddon family reunion in Alexandria, Virginia, in August 1998 to give a short talk and conduct a workshop on African American quilts. After his talk, several family members told him that their elders had passed along fragments of family stories to them, but they were cautioned as very young children not to share them with anyone. Remembered fragments of stories quickly fade. None of the people at the family reunion could remember specifically what their elders had been telling them; all they could remember was the need to maintain family secrets. On other occasions, the elders would chase the children from the rooms, saying, "This is not for you to hear."

This need for secrecy is understandable when we consider that from the time of slavery until today secrecy was one way the black community could protect itself. If the white man didn't know what was going on, he couldn't seek reprisals. Secrecy appears to be wedded to protection and becomes a matter of family honor. You do not tell strangers what is kept sacred to the family. If an elder binds you to secrecy on his or her deathbed, you never break that bond. Racial hostility and mistrust work hand in hand to keep things secret.

Secrets appear to be sewn into two of the most famous Bible quilts the quilt world has known. Drawing from Bible stories and natural phenomena, former slave Harriet Powers left two appliqué quilts that have provided scholars with many clues about African American quiltmaking in general and in particular her own perspective on life. Make no mistake about it: Powers's images have baffled many. There remains much to glean from her quilts. Exactly all that Powers is stating remains a mystery, a part of her secret world. These quilts may be the visual equivalent of the oral traditions of her people, pieced in fabric. What was she documenting?

Harriet Powers was born a slave in Athens, Georgia, in 1837. Her legacy consists of two "Bible story" quilts, one now exhibited at the Boston Fine Arts Museum, the other at the Smithsonian, as well as a photo of herself. It is generally agreed that the quilts depict cosmological events, such as those of May 19, 1780, when smoke from forest fires in New England caused the sky to go dark, and November 13, 1833, when a meteor storm lasted for eight hours. The quilts are appliquéd in much the same manner that some African textiles were appliquéd; each square telling a particular story.

For our purposes, there are two important observations about the quilts. Researchers have already concluded that Powers's quilts are historically accurate in terms of the cosmological events she depicts in some of the squares. Regenia A. Perry, professor emerita of African and African American art history at Virginia Commonwealth University, has theorized in her book *Harriet Powers's Bible Quilts*, that the many stars on the quilts represent constellations. There is strong precedent for this. As we have mentioned, the Pawnee and other Native American populations were known for their star maps. Could not Powers's quilt also be a coded star map, in which she was mapping the heavens as well, perhaps as a commemoration of Tubman's instructions to escaping slaves to "follow the North Star"? Was Powers also documenting the Underground Railroad as she had been told about it? Because Powers created her Bible quilts between the 1880s and '90s, what she depicts are stories and accounts told to her. Although much has been written about her Bible quilts, very little is known about the only existing photo of Powers herself. In the photo she is wearing a long white apron with saw-toothed edges. There are three appliquéd motifs on the apron: a moon, a cross, and a sun or shooting star. In her left hand, Powers holds a dark appliquéd patch that she points to with her right forefinger. Maude Wahlman suggests that the apron is "ceremonial" and that Powers was a member of a secret society or fraternal organization of some sort, the apron showing her status in the organization. Art historian Perry sees the apron as a "dress apron" that Southern women wear on special occasions. Raymond views the apron as the equivalent of a minister's robe, a religious article of clothing, and on several occasions when he has shown the slide of Harriet Powers to quilters' groups around the country, women from the audience have stated with certainty that the star on Powers's apron is indeed representative of the Eastern Star, the women's arm of the Masons.

We believe it was highly probable that Powers was a member of a secret organization, such as the Eastern Star. The first Grand Lodge, Savannah, Georgia, was established in 1870. For a Grand Lodge to be established, several smaller units, or lodges, would have to have existed throughout the state prior to this. In addition to Masonic Lodges, many other beneficial or mutual aid societies and fraternal organizations were proliferating in the South at this time. It is not unlikely that Powers was a member of one of these. We suspect that some of these same organizations, those dating back to the early to mid–nineteenth century, were instrumental in providing shelter and directions to other safe houses and the way north.

Providing directions to the fugitives was essential if the escape was to be a success. If "Follow the Drinking Gourd" provided specific directions for the slaves to move, other spirituals incorporated warning signals as well as instructions on how to go. "Wade in the Water" is just such a spiritual, according to Charles Blockson (1994) and others. Blockson contends that the song was sung as a warning to alert escaping slaves that the

bloodhounds were released to find them, and that they should go to the
water, whether a stream or a river, and travel along its banks so that the
dogs would have no scent to follow. Other slaves might issue the warning
to comrades already in flight. They probably were located on a nearby
plantation within hearing range of the fugitives passing by. Given the
"grape-vine" inter-plantation communication system, the slaves would
have been aware of an escape attempt and would learn of the hounds' re-
lease. Singing "Wade in the Water" would alert their fellow fugitives to
the danger and tell them what action to take. John Lovell writes that
Harriet Tubman sang "Wade in the Water" precisely to warn her charges
to "wade" or "walk" on the river's edge so the bloodhounds couldn't trace
their path. The song reads:

Chorus:

Wade in the water,

Wade in the water children.

Wade in the water,

God's gonna trouble the water.

See dat host all dressed in white,

God's gonna trouble the water;

The leader looks like the Israelite,

God's gonna trouble the water.

See dat ban' all dressed in red,

God's gonna trouble the water;

Looks like de ban dat Moses lead,

God's gonna trouble the water.

On another level, "Wade in the Water" was part of instructional singing,
according to other writers. In this case, the singing of the spiritual was a

signal to leave the plantation and meet at a designated place to begin the journey toward freedom. In this way, "Wade in the Water," when sung in concert with other spirituals, and accompanied by the naming of particular quilt patterns, was part of a verbal-visual communication system for the Underground Railroad.

When singing "Wade in the Water," escaping slaves could have drawn strength from the Old Testament story of God's intervention, God's troubling the waters of the pool of Bethesda, which is believed to be the source of the spiritual. The story tells of God sending an angel to touch a pool of still water, disturbing it by imbuing it with curative powers. When the people who were gathered in waiting saw the water form ripples, they believed it to be a sign of divine intervention and immediately jumped in, with the hope of being freed from their physical afflictions. Only the first ones in were cured. The others had to patiently wait until the next angelic visitation when God would again trouble the water (John 5:1–4).

Harriet Powers's appliquéd quilts, Peg Leg Joe's admonition to "follow the drinkin' gourd," and the Underground Railroad Quilt Code corroborate the admonition to "follow the stars." For guidance, they looked to the heavens, to the stars to chart their way. They fixed their gaze upon the North Star and followed it. They used this heavenly "drinking gourd" with the hope of eventually "tasting" the waters of freedom.

Spirituals taken as a whole contain a record and a revelation
of the deeper thoughts and experiences of the Negro in this country
for a period beginning three hundred years ago and covering
two and a half centuries. If you wish to know what they are
you will find them written more plainly in these songs
than in any pages of history.

JAMES WELDON JOHNSON,
AS QUOTED IN *WADE IN THE WATER*
by Arthur C. Jones

Chapter Seven

Steal Away

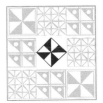

SPIRITUALS WERE MUCH MORE THAN PIOUS PRAISES OR SOULFUL lamentations sung by slaves and their descendants in response to the evils of bondage. Spirituals were the audio portion of a sophisticated system of communication on the Underground Railroad. The words, the refrains, the "call and response" method of singing, and even the rhythmic sounds produced by dancing feet contained a hidden meaning which only the trained ear could detect. That spirituals had double meanings is well proved by the published research of John Lovell, John Blassingame, Arthur Jones, Samuel Floyd, and others. Their recorded statements and other rich sources of oral history enable us to appreciate spirituals on more than one level.

Heritage lives via the spoken as well as the written word. African American family stories and secrets, passed down from generation to generation, reinforce the cultural stitches that bind a people and inform history. Ozella called upon oral tradition as she walked in the footsteps of her ancestors and explained to us that the singing and humming of particular spirituals accompanied the displaying of special quilts hung on clotheslines and fences. Together, the singing of spirituals and the displaying of quilts formed an audiovisual method of communication known only to certain slaves.

Spirituals did not float down from heaven. Instead, they rose out of African "ring rituals," African American "ring shouts," and the experience of slavery. In Africa, ring rituals were an integral part of religious expression, combining dance, drum, and song in order to manifest the union between the material and spiritual worlds (Floyd, p. 19). Each element in this trinity had its unique role to play. Dance, for example, was a way of generating or increasing what Samuel A. Floyd terms *ache*. *Ache*, according to African rite scholars, is the life force that pulsates through the body. This life force manifests itself in the passion with which the ring shout is performed. Their bodies were swaying to the rhythms of the drum and moving through space and time. The dancers moved without limitations. The drum was so powerful that it could speak to the dancer's soul as well as carry messages to distant places. Dancing in a ring formation affirmed communal solidarity and provided an opportunity to be free of all internal pressure. Slaves brought this ritual to America and adapted it to suit their new situation (Floyd, pp. 19–21).

In America, the ring ritual gives birth to the ring shout. The ring shout was also known as "shout," "glory shout," "holy dance," and "walk in Egypt," as noted by Floyd in *The Power of Black Music*. The ring shout was choreographed using African ring rituals and slave songs, or spirituals as they came to be called. Ring shouts were observed by many nineteenth-century visitors to the South and described to friends and relatives in letters. Lydia Parrish especially took interest in this uniquely African form of dance. In her groundbreaking work *Slave Songs of the Georgia Sea Islands*, Parrish gives her twentieth-century interpretation of the dance. She describes how the black Sea Islanders, descendants of slaves, would tap their heels on the floor of their church to imitate the beat of the drums their ancestors had been forbidden to use. Parrish actually recorded the sounds of this heel tapping and played it for her friends. The sound was indistinguishable from the sounds a drum would have made.

What Parrish and others describe seems to be a form of what we now term tap dancing. Is the ring ritual the precursor to tap dancing? Was tap dancing itself a form of coded communication, similar to Morse code? Musical critic and analyst Michael Ventura in his superb article on the history of African American music, "Hear That Long Snake Moan," states, "Except in New Orleans, slaves were not allowed to gather in groups, even for entertainment. Again, except in New Orleans, drums were forbidden. In place of drumming, North American slaves developed what we now know as tap dancing, but the loss of the drum meant the loss of their ceremonies."

Spirituals, like quilt patterns, migrated from location to location. Hearing the songs at one plantation, slaves would take them back to their own. With each movement the songs took on local dialects, words, and phrasing. The authors of *Slave Songs of the United States* (Allen, Ware, and Garrison) discuss hearing a song on Captain John Fripp's Southern plantation in the winter of 1863–64 and not hearing it again until the following spring at Coffin's Point, five miles away. While the song was basically the same, it had been altered only a bit. This proved that slaves, despite not being allowed to travel at will, maintained a covert method of communication that helped ensure cultural survival.

What were originally known as slave songs became "spirituals." By most accounts, the coining of the name "spiritual" happened in South

Carolina. In her book *Slave Songs of the Georgia Sea Islands*, Lydia Parrish cites the history of the spiritual. She writes that the term "spirituals" belonged to songs collected in South Carolina prior to 1909. She states that the word was not used in Hampton's *Cabin and Plantation* songs published in 1909. The word did not appear in Barton's *Old Plantation Hymns* of 1898 either. The first application of the term spirituals was in 1909 on St. Catherine's Island, an island halfway between the Savannah River and the Altamaha. "Spirituals" was the name adopted by slaves of South Carolina and Georgia (Parrish, xxvii). The word took hold and moved first to North Carolina, then farther northward and westward, until the country as a whole began calling the religious songs of the slaves spirituals. Spirituals became the common language, the verbal expression of slavery, joining together the voices of black slaves throughout the South and elsewhere.

Ozella told us that spirituals were sung to instruct on everything—when to leave, where to go, and what to look for along the journey to the promised land, to Canaan/Canada.

In his expanded autobiography of 1855, *My Bondage and My Freedom,* Frederick Douglass writes that singing was a necessity on the plantation. Not only was singing during daily as well as religious activity an African tradition, but singing was also essential to the field slave who had to prove his/her industriousness to the suspicious plantation overseer. Silence was not an option. Slaves would admonish each other to "make a noise" and "bear a hand." The teams of field workers would sing so that the overseer might know where they were (Douglass, p. 97).

When reminiscing about a childhood experience of witnessing a group of slaves singing boisterously as they walked through the woods returning from a hard day's work, Douglass addresses a paradox inherent in the spirituals. He writes that the loud sounds, though seeming to express pure joy, were muted by a strain of melancholy. He further comments that these sounds were interpreted by the overseer and master to be a joyful noise made unto the Lord. That "noise" contained something very powerful, however. According to Douglass, the slaves would embellish what he called hymns with "improvised jargon": jargon that had no discernible meaning to others, not even to the young Douglass. He noticed, nevertheless, that the jargon appeared to be filled with meaning to his fellow slaves (Douglass, p. 98). This jargon merits comparison to the "speaking in tongues" of the ring shout. In both cases, what was perceived to be nonsense sounds by the master could easily and most shrewdly have been a mixture of African dialects forming a coded language known only to the "initiated" or educated ear. Not every slave would be privy to the meaning. Only those who were proved trustworthy and taken into the confidence of the plantation grapevine would have understood what they were hearing.

In what may be reference to those strange "sounds" overheard by young Douglass, folklorist Frank Dobie (1928) counts among his favorite spirituals a song simply entitled "A Song." Dobie states that when he heard the song sung, its words "sound like a vivid but unintelligible description of a battle or a cyclone. It is of the nature of a call—like a yodel to the Swiss mountaineer." The song is obviously of African origin.

The "sounds" comprising the spirituals communicated secrets while girding those who were about to escape with courage, determination, and faith. Frederick Douglass makes this clear when he writes that he and his five male companions repeatedly sang:

> O Canaan, sweet Canaan,
> I am bound for the land of Canaan.

Douglass leaves no doubt that he and his companions were not referring to heaven. They were singing about the North, about their Canaan. Soon,

Canada replaced the North as the Land of Canaan due to the strengthen-
ing of the fugitive slave laws and the weakening of the North's position as
a safe place.

Douglass was fond of other spirituals that were considered to be sub-
versive by Southern slaveholders. Often cited, one of these spirituals
reads:

> A few more beatings of the wind and rain,
>
> Ere the winter will be over—
>
> Glory, Hallelujah!
>
> Some friends has gone before me
>
> I must try to go and meet them—
>
> Glory, Hallelujah!
>
> A few more risings and settings of the sun,
>
> Ere the winter will be over—
>
> Glory, Hallelujah!
>
> There's a better day a coming—
>
> There's a better day a coming—
>
> Oh, Glory, Hallelujah!

The threat this spiritual posed is best expressed in the words of former slave Charity Bowery, who is cited in several publications. Referring
to the spiritual, Bowery states: "They wouldn't let us sing that. They
thought we was going to rise, because we sung 'better days are coming.'"
Charity describes the tense atmosphere of the 1830s:

> The brightest and best men were killed in Nat's time. Such ones
> are always suspected. All the colored folks were afraid to pray in
> the time of old Prophet Nat. There was no law about it; but the
> Whites reported it round among themselves that, if a note was
> heard, we should have some dreadful punishment; and after that,

the low Whites would fall upon any slaves they heard praying or singing a hymn, and often killed them before their masters or mistresses could get to them. (Child, pp. 42–43; Epstein, p. 229)

Hysteria swept across the South after the insurrections of Denmark Vesey in 1822 in Charleston and Nat Turner in 1831 in southeastern Virginia. Filled with anxiety, Southern whites blamed black preachers and the distinctive religious songs of the slaves, the spirituals, for inspiring the revolts. One poignant example is a speech that Governor Floyd of Virginia delivered to the state legislature in 1831. The governor requested that tougher laws be passed against "the most active incendiaries . . . , the ne-gro preachers." He went on to insist that unless a white person was in at-tendance, the weekday religious meetings by slaves should be outlawed in the name of public interest and "that the negro preachers be silenced" (Epstein, p. 229, and *Journal of the Senate of Virginia,* 1831, pp. 9–10).

Despite the threat of recriminations, slaves, including Douglass, con-tinued to sing the spirituals. The oppressive atmosphere of intolerance and suspicion made secrecy and coded communication a necessity. This was accomplished through the clever use of everyday objects. One well-known example involves turning a cooking pot upside down to signal a meeting that night. According to folklore, the inverted pot would contain the sounds of the meeting, ensuring secrecy. The simple words of a spir-itual take on added significance. Douglass explains how outsiders would interpret a song literally, but the slaves would understand the hidden meaning. The example he gives is the following.

I thought I heard them say,
There were lions in the way.
I don't expect to stay
Much longer here.

> Run to Jesus—shun the danger—
> I don't expect to stay
> Much longer here.
> (D o u g l a s s , p . 2 7 9)

Douglass tells us that these verses were interpreted by outsiders as expectations of a quick journey to the realm of the Spirit. While that could be the original intended meaning of the song, in special circumstances the verses expressed a "speedy pilgrimage" toward a free state and deliverance from all the evils and dangers of slavery.

Douglass shares how and by whom the "pilgrimage" was realized. He describes nightly secret meetings and Sunday encounters as times when he and his companions discussed all aspects, especially the consequences, of their proposed escape. According to Miles Mark Fisher, the author of *Negro Slave Songs in the United States,* these secret meetings were called by singing the following familiar communion hymn, "Let Us Break Bread Together."

> Let us break bread together on our knees,
> Let us break bread together on our knees.
> When I fall on my knees, with my face to the rising sun,
> O Lord, have mercy on me!
>
> Let us drink wine together on our knees,
> Let us drink wine together on our knees.
> When I fall on my knees, with my face to the rising sun,
> O Lord, have mercy on me!
>
> Let us praise God together on our knees,
> Let us praise God together on our knees.

When I fall on my knees, with my face to the rising sun,
O Lord, have mercy on me!

(A r t h u r   C. J o n e s,   p.   4 5)

Douglass admits to the use of secret codes or "pass words" as he calls them. These were necessary to safeguard communication between him and his men while in the presence of others. He writes: "I hated the secrecy, but where slavery is powerful, and liberty is weak, the latter is driven to concealment or to destruction" (Douglass, p. 280).

Spirituals would serve as the form of concealment. Douglass is not the only source of information for researchers. Other published slave autobiographies, some slave narratives, and letters have aided scholars in their understanding of spirituals. The pioneering collaborative work of William Allen, Charles Ware, and Lucy McKim Garrison, published as *Slave Songs of the United States* in 1867, serves as a most valuable adjunct. Thanks to this early anthology, modern scholars like Blassingame, Blockson, and Floyd are able to advance our knowledge of the spirituals. Lydia Parrish's fieldwork on the Sea Islands is also a significant contribution to our understanding.

In one of his numerous publications, Charles Blockson singles out the spiritual "Steal Away" as an obvious example of the instruction type. The song's admonition to steal away to Jesus was also a directive to run away to freedom. The song reads:

Chorus:
Steal away, steal away,
Steal away to Jesus.
Steal away, steal away,
I ain't got long to stay here.

My Lord calls me, He calls me by the thunder
Green trees are bending, poor sinner stands a trembling
Tombstones are bursting, poor sinner stands a trembling
My Lord calls me, He calls me by the lightning

The trumpet sounds within a my soul,
I ain't got long to stay here.

There are several key words and phrases here. "He calls me by the
thunder" is interpreted by several writers as an indication to leave during a rainstorm. To do so would ensure that the dogs would have no
scent to pick up and that any footprints would be washed away.
Thunderstorms tend to take place in spring or in autumn when the seasons are changing. "Green trees bending" is a sign of springtime.
Ozella also identified springtime as the season when the slave left the
plantation. The song's reference to "tombstones" might literally identify a grave site, perhaps the slave grave site where many night burials
and secret meetings were held. Remember that the Appalachian, Blue
Ridge, and Allegheny mountain ranges have foot trails snaking through
them. Many of these trails, moving south to north as well as east to
west, became escape routes.

The slaves were called to escape to the mountains. They heeded the
call. The tension incurred by running away must have heightened the
drama of a storm in the mountains. Given the biblical allusions, the whole
event must have seemed apocalyptic to the fugitives. Lightning illuminated
the landscape so that those escaping might recognize landmarks and
therefore know where they are, yet the strobelike flashes were not of such
duration as to give the slaves away.

An old Southern admonition, one that Raymond heard often as a
child in his grandmother's presence, states that you must sit still and be

silent because God is speaking through the thunder. The thunder was God's voice. The voice in the spiritual was forcefully saying, "Run, run away. When you hear the roar of thunder, run toward the mountains. The rain will wash away your tracks." Inspiration, courage, and anxiety all coursed through the veins of those running to freedom. They were compelled by a trumpet sounding within their souls. They would no longer remain in slavery. They would be free.

Thunder, lightning, and trumpets within the soul describe the turbulent spirit of Nat Turner, the mystic, prophet, and revolutionary who believed himself to be elected by Divine Providence to make a lasting mark upon the earth. Turner was born in Southampton County, Virginia, on October 2, 1800. From the very early years of his life, he was aware of his disquieted spirit. His childhood circumstances and adolescent years were somewhat similar to those of Harriet Tubman and to a lesser degree Frederick Douglass. Turner was the youngest of these three powerful leaders. His self-image and approach to life was largely determined by a literal interpretation of the Bible. All three saw themselves as liberators who were inspired by stories from the Old Testament to lead their people to freedom. Others, swayed by their inspiration, followed them.

Since childhood, Turner experienced what he termed visions, and he declared having heard heavenly voices commanding him to fight evil, to battle against the Serpent that took the form of slavery. His testimony, given to writer Thomas Gray, bears witness to all of his extraordinary spiritual experiences. Gray described Turner as exceptional in his awareness of his mission, and able to speak lucidly about them. Like Joan of Arc or the angel dispatched by God to visit death upon the firstborn of the Egyptians as punishment for not heeding the words of Moses and freeing the enslaved Israelites, Turner saw himself as God's agent. Turner would deliver God's wrath upon the slaveholders, visiting upon them what they had visited upon the enslaved. He led a violent insurrection, exacting an "eye for an eye" in the battle to set his people free.

Floyd J. Coleman, a respected scholar of African and African American art, reminds us that Shango, the Yoruba god of the storm, is manifested as thunder and lightning. Like Shango, Turner metaphorically caused "thunder axes," the instruments of Shango, to rain down from heaven when he killed the slaveholders, using an axe. As in the Nigerian story of Shango, Turner would steal away into the woods after he struck. It is said that Turner used the spiritual "Steal Away" to summon his troops to secret meetings, and some spiritual specialists such as Arthur Jones have proposed that Turner was, in fact, the composer of "Steal Away."

Although Turner's insurrection ultimately failed, his actions demonstrated that a revolt was possible. Word about his partial success, his bravery, and his prophetic mission moved swiftly through the slave population from plantation to plantation, inspiring many. The legend of Nat Turner was born. Slaves would celebrate Turner in stories and in song.

To the plantation owners and most Southern whites, the name Nat Turner became synonymous with danger, evil, and a threat to their way of life. They hated and feared him as much in death as they did in life. As such, trouble greeted any slave who mentioned the name of Nat Turner. This prohibition was circumvented through the manipulation of words in conversation and in song. Note how clearly disguised is the message in the following song.

> You might be a Carroll from Carrollton,
> Arrive here night afo' Lawd made creation,
> But you can't keep the world from moverin' around
> And *not turn her* back from the gaining ground.

As Jones notes, the italicized phrase, "not turn her," is a reference to Nat Turner. This song would be sung over and over again, both to make fun of the aristocratic Carroll family and to keep alive the story of Turner's insurrection.

The vaguely disguised Turner song, the Douglass-designed code, and many spirituals are like the Underground Railroad Quilt Code in that all are examples of an enslaved people crafting their own system of conveying messages and instructions on escape tactics. Canada was the ultimate destination. Canada for the young Douglass was a relatively unknown place which he calls the land to where wild geese would fly at winter's end. Indeed, geese fly north during springtime and fly south during the fall. This natural phenomenon provided direction and an observable time schedule for those seeking to leave the South. The geese would rest by ponds and small lakes, making a noise that was audible for miles. This informed the fugitives of the whereabouts of fresh water.

Leaving the plantation was comparable to troubling the still waters of their lives as slaves risked severe punishment or even death as retribution for their escape. Nevertheless, they troubled the waters and took flight, believing God would help them.

Relating once again to the Old Testament story of Moses leading his people to the promised land, Harriet Tubman, the most famous of the Underground Railroad conductors, was known as the Moses of her people for her similar work. It is said that Denmark Vesey, a free black in Charleston, in 1822 also took as his inspiration for insurrection the story of Moses as well as his knowledge of the slave uprisings in Haiti. Vesey is said to have read biblical accounts of the children of Israel at every meeting with his followers (Harding, p. 69). Some scholars even credit Vesey as the writer of the hymn "Go Down, Moses." Both Vesey and, later, Tubman took seriously the biblical injunction to "Let my people go."

Harriet Tubman, the most famous conductor on the Underground Railroad. (Courtesy Howard University, Moorland Spingarn Collection)

Frederick Douglass (Detail of engraving courtesy Howard University, Moorland Spingarn Collection)

What inspiration for the followers in singing these words from "Go Down, Moses":

> When Israel was in Egypt land,
> Let my people go;
> Oppressed so hard they could not stand,
> Let my people go.

> "Thus saith the Lord," bold Moses said,
> "Let my people go;
> If not, I'll smite your first-born dead,
> Let my people go!"

> *Chorus:*
> O go down, Moses
> Away down to Egypt's land
> And tell King Pharaoh
> To let my people go!

The verses go on to number twenty-four in all, with references to Canaan, the wilderness, and means of travel. The following are the last three verses of the spiritual, which appeared in the *National Anti-Slavery Standard 22* on December 21, 1861:

> We need not always weep and mourn,
> O let my people go!
> And wear these Slavery chains forlorn,
> O let my people go!

> This world's a wilderness of woe,
> O let my people go!

O let us on to Canaan go,
O let my people go!

What a beautiful morning that will be!
O let my people go!
When time breaks up in eternity,
O let my people go!

(Epstein, pp. 363-65)

Harriet Tubman, Underground Railroad conductor, nurse, spy, and scout, was a short woman of dark complexion whose looks and demeanor were ordinary, but whose faith, courage, tenacity, wit, ingenuity, and generosity positioned her far above the average. She embodied the extraordinary within the ordinary and was able to hide much in plain view. She used simple disguises, the sunbonnet hiding her face being the most famous one, to prevent identification, and she turned to song as a primary means of communication. In Tubman's own words, recorded by biographer Sarah H. Bradford, we learn about her use of spirituals.

Tubman was so fond of spirituals that she composed some of her own. She loved to sing and she frequently communicated through song. She sang loudly as she walked past the dwellings of her friends and relatives on the night before she ran away for the first time. Nothing inhibited her, not even encountering the plantation owner as she headed for the gate. To throw him off, Tubman sang all the louder. She tells us how the master looked back at her, puzzled by what he heard. He must have been suspicious, and with good reason. Tubman was gone by morning. Her farewell song reads:

Slave cabins on slave row, Boone Hall Plantation, Charleston, South Carolina. These cabins are made of brick and wood. (Photographed by Raymond G. Dobard)

Log Cabin quilt "airing" in window of slave cabin. This quilt is "hidden in plain view." Boone Hall Plantation, Charleston, South Carolina. (Quiltmaker/ photographed by Raymond G. Dobard)

Log Cabin quilt on fence bearing the double light and dark pattern arrangement. (Quiltmaker/photographed by Raymond G. Dobard)

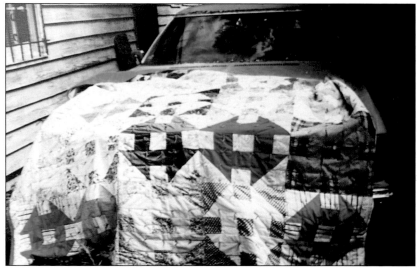

Reproduction of McDaniel family photo of Monkey Wrench quilt made by Ozella's mother. This quilt would have been the first quilt exhibited by the head seamstress; it directed the slaves to get their tools/belongings together in preparation to escape. (Photographed by Raymond G. Dobard)

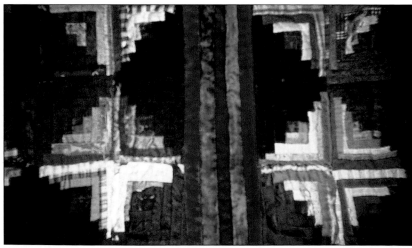

An exceptional example of an early log cabin quilt that was made by a fugitive slave woman in the 1840s and was carried to Canada as a gift for William King, founder of the Elgin Settlement in Buxton, Ontario, a region known for its large population of free blacks. Harriet Tubman, Frederick Douglass, and John Brown met in Chatham, a town in the vicinity of Buxton. (Photo courtesy of the Buxton Museum)

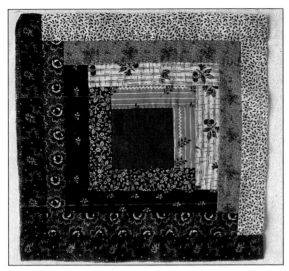

*The Log Cabin pattern,
late-nineteenth-century
block. (Collection/
photographed by
Raymond G. Dobard)*

*Log Cabin variation. This quilt comes from Georgia and is said to be slave-made.
The date is given as c. 1830s by its owner, Ms. Janice Stutts of Carrollton, Georgia.
The quilt measures 66 by 70 1/ 2 inches. The backing fabric measures 22 inches wide
per panel. The width of fabric helps us to date quilts because the older fabrics are less
wide than today's. (Collection/photograph courtesy of Ms. Janice Stutts)*

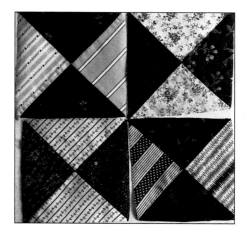

This pattern is known as Bow Tie, Hourglass, and Pinwheel. These patterns are made from one unit. Look carefully and you will see that the Hourglass is a vertical arrangement of triangles; the Bow Tie is the horizontal placement; and the Pinwheel is the pattern hidden in the center of this design. Hourglass patterns arranged to form a pinwheel center. (Collection/photographed by Raymond G. Dobard)

Flying Geese pattern. In this example the four sets of triangles point in four different directions. Moving clockwise from top right to bottom, the triangles

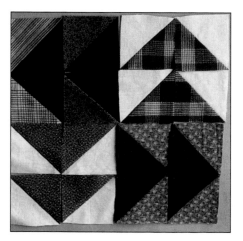

point north, east, south, and west. The fabric selection in this example distinguishes the triangles in the upper left-hand corner, promoting a western direction. (Made and photographed by Raymond G. Dobard)

Drunkard's Path pattern encouraged the slaves to follow a zigzag path similar to the staggering gait of a drunk. The Africans believed that evil traveled only in straight lines. There is believed to be a connection between that superstition and the quilt pattern. It is also interesting to note that the safe houses were staggered for protective reasons as well. (Collection/photographed by Raymond G. Dobard)

Evening Stars by the Morning Light Quilt made by Raymond G. Dobard. Since the escaping slaves were told to follow the North Star, many nineteenth-century quilts contain star images. (Photographed by Raymond G. Dobard)

Jacob's Ladder. This example dates to the 1880s. This design is based upon the biblical story of Jacob and enjoys a long and fascinating history. Early Jacob's Ladder quilts are either blue and white or red and white. A third, intermediary color was added later when the pattern was changed. Jacob's Ladder can have three or five rungs in abstracted form. A variation of this pattern was called Railroad Crossing in 1831, according to Ruth Finley (see Finley, p. 71). (Collection/ photographed by Raymond G. Dobard)

The Plantation Quilt by Mrs. Elizabeth Talford Scott features a constellation of stars in various shapes and sizes. This quilt is a replica of a quilt that Mrs. Scott owned as a youth. The original was lost in a fire. In this portion the intricate quilting adds dimension and is believed to be a detail of a plantation. (Photographed by Elizabeth T. Scott)

Detail of 1980 Plantation Quilt made by Elizabeth Talford Scott. Detailed stitching surrounds the star motifs, forming what appears to be a topographical map. (Photograph courtesy of Elizabeth T. Scott)

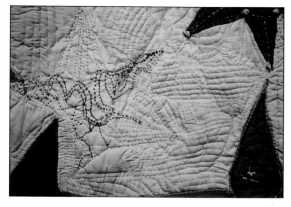

Sampler quilt, pieced together in 1987-88 by members of the Daughters of Dorcas and Sons of Washington, D.C., that includes a number of patterns in the code. Note the Monkey Wrench, Nine Patch, Evening Star, and Pinwheel patterns. (Collection/photographed by Raymond G. Dobard)

Tumbling Blocks. This pattern is called Tumbling Boxes by Ozella McDaniel Williams and is identified by her as the tenth pattern of the code. The pattern is also known as Baby Blocks and is celebrated for its three-dimensional appearance. To piece this pattern, one must be an advanced quiltmaker. (Quiltmaker/photographed by Raymond G. Dobard)

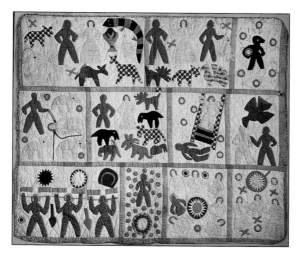

Harriet Powers's Bible Quilt. This famous 1886 African American narrative appliqué quilt celebrates scenes from Scripture. This was the first Bible quilt made by Harriet Powers (1837-1911). The Bible quilt is the grandmother of today's story quilts. (National Museum of Natural History, Smithsonian Institution, Washington, D.C.)

Harriet Powers's Pictorial Quilt. This is the second quilt that Powers created and dates to 1895-98. It is unusual in that it contains not only scenes from Scripture but also depictions of natural phenomena, such as the Leonid meteor storm of c. 1833, an event that Powers heard about, since it happened before she was born. Powers takes the opportunity here to "preach" through her choice of people and events depicted. (Bequest of Maxim Karolik. Courtesy of the Museum of Fine Arts, Boston)

I'm sorry I'm gwine to lebe you,
Farewell, oh farewell;
But I'll meet you in the mornin',
Farewell, oh farewell.

I'll meet you in the mornin',
I'm boun' for de promised land,
On the oder side of Jordan,
Boun' for de promised land.

I'll meet you in the mornin',
Safe in de promised land,
On the oder side of Jordan,
Boun' for de promised land.

(Bradford, 1869, pp. 18-19)

Indeed, Tubman was bound for the promised land. Once there, she worked hard in order to make return visits to bring others out of bondage. That was her mission. She became the Moses of her people, leading hundreds to freedom.

On her journeys, Tubman used songs to indicate when it was safe for the fugitives to move from place to place. She also warned her charges of encroaching danger through the use of song. In her own words, Tubman explained how this system worked. She told Sarah Bradford that she instructed her "passengers" to hide in the woods during the day while she went to the home of a friend of the Underground Railway, as she called it, to buy needed provisions. She could not return to her charges until nightfall, lest she be discovered and lead slave catchers back to the hiding place. The song that Tubman would sing as an all-clear sign was one she composed herself. It was sung to a simple Methodist melody, Bradford writes. The song reads:

Hail, oh hail ye happy spirits,
Death no more shall make you fear,
No grief nor sorrow, pain nor anger [anguish]
Shall no more distress you there.

Around him are ten thousan' angels
Always ready to 'bey comman'.
Dey are always hobring round you,
Till you reach the hebbenly lan'.

Jesus, Jesus will go wid you;
He will lead you to his throne;
He who died has gone before you,
Trod de wine-press all alone.

He whose thunder shake creation;
He who bids the planets roll;
He who rides above the temple [tempest]
An' his scepter sways the whole.

Dark and thorny is the desert
Through the pilgrim makes his ways,
Yet beyon' dis vale of sorrow,
Lies de fiel's of endless days.

Tubman discloses the way she used her song, her spiritual, saying:

De first time I go by singing dis hymn, dey don't come out to me
. . . til I listen if de coast is clar; den when I go back and sing it
again, dey come out. But if I sing:

Moses go down in Egypt,
Tell ole Pharo' let my people go;
Hadn't ben for Adam' fall,
Shouldn't hab to died at all.

den dey don't come out, for dere's danger in de way. (Bradford,
1869, p. 27)

What a chilling experience it must have been for all as they waited,
exhausted, hungry, and in a constant state of anxiety, hoping to hear the
lengthy spiritual sung twice.

The spiritual that Tubman enjoyed the most, according to Blockson
and others, was "Swing Low Sweet Chariot." We are told that this spiritual was sung by her friends in tribute to her on the evening of her death,
March 10, 1913 (Blockson, 1994, p. 338).

It is not surprising that "Swing Low Sweet Chariot" was Harriet
Tubman's favorite song. The words draw from the Old Testament accounts
of Elijah and Ezekiel in which the chariot figures prominently. Just as it did
for Elijah, the blazing chariot waited for Tubman and for all champions of
God and of the oppressed. The biblical chariot takes the just to glory. In
the spirituals, the chariot symbolizes a means of transportation, a wagon,
or a conductor of the Underground Railroad. Of the many spirituals in
which the chariot motif appears, Samuel Floyd (p. 214) cites the following:

Swing Low Sweet Chariot
Swineter Ride Up in de Chariot Soon a in de Mornin'
Great Day
Up on de Mountain
De Band o'Gideon
Zekiel Saw de Wheel

God New, de Chariot's Comin'
Oh Wasn't Dat a Wide Riber
He's the Lily of the Valley
March On
Tell It

Floyd analyzes the chariot trope, as he calls it, in seventeen printed anthologies of spirituals that were published between 1867 and 1933. Eleven spirituals contain the word "chariot" in their titles, and in twenty-three more the word appears in the text. Summarizing the songs, Floyd writes:

> In these songs, the chariot variously will "swing low" to pick up and carry the slaves home, to ride the singers up "over Jordan." It brings peace, rest, and release from the secular world. It is "good news" that "the chariot's coming" to allow the slaves to "trabble on" to heaven. The chariot of the songs is sometimes one in which "King Jesus" rides, being pulled by "four white horses side by side." It rides across the sky and "stops," which means "good news" for the righteous. At other times, the chariot, rather than flying, "rolls along," pulled this time by "twelve white horses," and it has only one or two wheels that run either "by faith" or "by the grace of God." (pp. 213–14)

The well-known spiritual reads:

Chorus:

Swing low sweet chariot,
Comin' for to carry me home,
Swing low sweet chariot,
Comin' for to carry me home.

Swing low sweet chariot
Comin' for to carry me home,
Swing low sweet chariot,
Comin' for to carry me home.

I look'd over Jordan, an' what did I see,
Comin' for to carry me home,
A band of angels comin' after me
Comin' for to carry me home.
(chorus)
You get a dere befo' I do,
Comin' for to carry me home,
Tell all my friends I'm comin' too,
Comin' for to carry me home.
(chorus)

The descriptive imagery of the "chariot songs" affords ample opportunity to devise coded instructions. Of the many images in these songs, the wheel emerges as having tremendous symbolic potential. The wheel alludes to many things, including wagons and the sun. Depending on the context in which the wheel is used, it can determine the time of day or indicate a direction. As we've discussed, the wheel also enjoys distinction as a popular nineteenth-century quilt pattern with various names such as Blazing Sun and Wheel of Fortune.

The chariot wheels rolled on in the nineteenth century until a faster means of transportation arrived. Carriages and wagons were common modes of transportation for the early century and were the "chariots" of the spirituals. The newly introduced railroad train, the "iron horse," was a chariot for the later part of the nineteenth century and was a bold new means of moving across the land at high speed. Within a short period of time, train imagery replaced the chariot in newly written spirituals. An example of this is the song entitled "The Gospel Train's a Comin'." The use of the word "train" initiated a new vocabulary and infused new metaphors into the language of the spiritual and the Underground Railroad. The Gospel Train quickly became a code name for the Underground Railroad. When this spiritual was sung, the slaves knew that a "conductor" was in their midst or that fugitives would be in the vicinity of the plantation that night, should anyone wish to escape. Another spiritual, "This Train Is Bound for Glory," was also sung in connection with Underground Railroad activity. However, instead of heaven, "glory" referred to freedom. The exchange of temporal for heavenly destinations was a common Underground Railroad ploy. But the slaves had to exercise some degree of caution when singing the train songs because the true meaning of the songs was easier to detect than the more cryptic biblically based chariot songs.

Poetic justice prevailed as trains and railway tracks came to serve the Underground Railroad and its passengers. Tubman provides a telling example of the train's use. Spirituals had accompanied her and the fugitives from the time of their departure from the plantation to the moment of their arrival in Canada. Tubman recalls how excited she and one of her parties of fugitives became upon crossing the upstate New York railroad suspension bridge. In the railway car, in the midst of strangers, Tubman and her charges broke into spontaneous song when they reached midbridge and the freedom line. From there they could glimpse Canada out of the train car window. With their sight fixed on the promised land and the thundering sounds of Niagara Falls as accompaniment, they sang:

I'm on the way to Canada,
That cold and dreary land,

De sad effects of slavery,

I can't no longer stand;

I've served my Master all my days,

Widout a dime reward,

And now I'm forced to run away,

To flee the lash abroad;

Farewell, ole Master, don't think hard of me,

I'm traveling on to Canada, where all de slaves are free.

De hounds are baying on my track,

Ole Master comes behind,

Resolved that he will bring me back.

Before I cross the line;

I'm now embarked for yonder shore,

Where a man's a man by law,

De iron horse will bear me o'er,

To "shake de lion's paw";

O righteous Father, wilt thou not pity me,

And help me on to Canada, where all de slaves are free.

Oh, I heard Queen Victoria say,

That if we would forsake,

Our native land of slavery,

And come across de lake;

Dat she was standing on de shore,

Wid arms extended wide,

To give us all a peaceful home,

Beyond the rolling tide;

Farewell, ole Master, don't think hard of me,

I'm traveling on to Canada, where all de slaves are free.

(Bradford, 1886, pp. 49-50)

Once on the shores of Canaan, on the free British soil of Canada, the fugitives sang:

> Glory to God in the highest,
>
> Glory to God and Jesus too,
>
> For all these souls now safe.

(B r a d f o r d , 1 8 8 6 , p. 5 2)

For these and the numerous others whom Harriet Tubman had guided, the passage on the suspension railroad bridge over water was a different kind of "Middle Passage." This passage carried them into freedom, not bondage. Finally they could be free men and women. Were it not for the spirituals working in concert with other secret methods of communication, Tubman and her charges would not have made it to the middle of the bridge linking Canada to America. How appropriate for a train to be one of the final forms of transportation. It was indeed the Gospel Train that carried them across.

Chapter Eight

African American Quilts:

Styles and Traditions

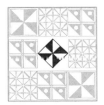

WE HAVE SEEN HOW GEOMETRIC PATTERNS, TIES, KNOTS, STITCHES, and color choices functioned together in early African American quilts as a means of conveying messages to escaping slaves. We now turn our attention to twentieth-century African American quilts to see what has happened to the quiltmaking techniques and design elements that helped deliver some slaves from bondage. Are the irregular stitches, visible knots, ties, bold colors, flickering patterns, strip piecing, and geometric work still used to transmit messages, or has the "freedom visual vocabulary" taken on new meaning? Are today's African American quilts, especially the utilitarian or improvisational quilts, the result of solely aesthetic decisions or the product of quiltmaking "as Grandma did it" without knowing why Great-Great-Grandma quilted as she did? Can the African textile influence still be detected in today's African American quilts? Is it possible that style has obliterated meaning? And what has happened to the metaphysical layer? Are African American quilts no longer empowered with special ties and knots, or with particular herbs placed in the batting? The many traditions of the early slave-made quilts have either disappeared or are hidden in new ways.

The answers come from several contemporary quilters whose works contain evidence of African narrative traditions. When comparing the past to the present, we must consider what has happened to the narrative quiltmaking tradition. Today story quilts and art quilts make up a new genre. Subjects ranging from African American fiction to community history and cultural celebrations are popular. The messages are overt, no longer invisibly stitched or subtly applied. Secrecy has given way to celebration and to ownership. The poetic ambiguity of the past bows to the prosaic illustrations of the present where mystery is diminished.

The story quilt and narrative art quilt, however, are the offspring of Harriet Powers's Bible quilts. Faith Ringgold, Michael Cummings, Carolyn Mazloomi, and Elizabeth Scott are four of the top African American quiltmakers of this new genre. They have not replaced the tradition of Harriet Powers as much as they have adapted and expanded it to meet their own artistic needs. These modern-day quilt artists join Powers in drawing from the appliqué heritage of the Fon artists of Africa's ancient Dahomey.

Faith Ringgold draws from family stories and African American history. In *Bitter Nest Part II: Harlem Renaissance Party* (1988), she recalls the events in the life of CeCe, a young deaf-mute Harlem resident who attended a dinner party in the 1920s with such Harlem Renaissance luminaries as Langston Hughes and W. E. B. Du Bois.

Stylistically, Ringgold frames her narrative with "strips" of text and a vibrant Hourglass/Bow Tie quilt pattern. Like the Dahomey artists, Ringgold tells the story of the struggle for achievement, but has portraits of prominent twentieth-century African American history makers instead of Dahomian symbolic representations of kings in animal or fish forms. Ringgold combines the geometric patterns with her central narrative as if she were framing the action with history. This is her method of placing the event "in context."

In addition to the pieced, painted, and printed fabric, Ringgold repeatedly uses the X design for quilting. Since her work is not heavily quilted, what quilting there is stands out prominently. Might we compare her use of the X with the *nsibidi* sign for "word" or the Kongo cosmogram indicating the four moments of the sun, a reference to the cycles of life? Ringgold, unlike some African American rural Southern quilters, is aware of her African heritage and draws from it consciously. By creating story quilts, Ringgold continues the African American narrative tradition, celebrating oral history through fabric.

The narrative vignettes of Michael Cummings owe much to the highly stylized, restructured or "pieced" images of Romare Bearden, the African American painter whose collage compositions are as compelling as the reductive figures of Harriet Powers. The storytelling ability of Bearden and the patchwork construction of his collages understandably appealed to the young Cummings in the 1980s.

Cummings's approach to quiltmaking is remarkably similar to Bearden's artistic style. Cummings employs minimal quilting in his compositions, preferring to focus upon the subjects of his work and their monumentality. Like Bearden and Ringgold, Cummings "teaches" about African American culture through his subject matter, as seen in his 1987 work *Haitian Boat People*.

Bearden and John Biggers were influenced by African American quiltmaking. A close viewing of Bearden's collages reveals that his way of "painting" has stronger stylistic and methodological ties to African American quiltmaking than it does to French Cubism. Bearden was so inspired by quiltmaking that he includes the word "quilt" in several of his titles and brilliantly employs several quiltmaking techniques to build, to piece, his images. Bearden, born in North Carolina, did not forget his Southern roots. He honored them by drawing on his memories to tell stories in his collages and paintings.

For the painter John Biggers, the stories surrounding African American quiltmaking, the ties to Africa, and the celebration of color within a given geometric matrix fuels his artistic drive and fills his large canvases as well as his murals. His work exhibits a prevalence of quiltmaking rituals and geometric patterns. Nowhere is this clearer than in his 1987 acrylic on canvas entitled *Starry Crown*. In this painting three women sit engaged in what appears to be a mystical quilting bee. Quilt patterns of Stars, Ocean Weaves, Hourglass/Bow Tie, Pinwheel, and checkerboards cover nearly every inch of the painting. The women represent the three Marys of the African American community who are the three cultures of ancient Africa: Egypt, Benin, and the Dogon of Mali (Wardlaw, p. 192). The central female figure represents the Dogon weaver of the "word," a storyteller who transmits knowledge across time and space through the spoken word. This seamstress sews tales, proverbs, and divine teachings into quilts. She wears a cultural crown, a starry crown, and a dress of many colors (Wardlaw, p. 192).

Color is of paramount importance to quilter-writer Dr. Carolyn Mazloomi of Cincinnati, Ohio, who founded the Women of Color Quilter's Network in the early 1980s in order to preserve and foster quilting among African Americans. Carolyn's own work is richly layered with African symbolism. In her wall quilt of 1991, entitled *The Water Brought Us Here . . . , The Water Will Take Us Back . . . ,* Carolyn addresses the painful subject of the Middle Passage and the role of a mother on board the ship. The central image of a mother and child rises out of the water in which small skeletons are floating. Carolyn, in keeping with other African American quiltmaking customs, has added shells, mirrors, and found objects to her quilt top. Like quilter Elizabeth Scott, Carolyn adds objects to the quilt top in order to empower the quilt. While the mother and child are depicted in bright colors, there is a profound sadness about the quilt. Perhaps the title is the triggering mechanism as it is taken from the legendary words of the Ibo people, who upon their arrival by slave ship in St. Simons Island, turned around and walked back into the water. Symbolically they were going back to Africa. In actuality they chose to drown rather than surrender themselves to slavery. Carolyn skillfully communicates this Ibo story that still haunts Gullah communities to this day.

Another African American founder of a quilt guild is Mrs. Viola Canady of Washington, D.C. Mrs. Canady, born in 1922, is a native of Goldsboro, North Carolina. When she retired from the Department of the Army, where for nineteen and a half years she served as tailor fitter in charge of the uniforms worn by the guards for the Tomb of the Unknown Soldier, Mrs. Canady returned to quilting. She then founded the Daughters of Dorcas in 1979 and embarked on a quilting career that took her to many parts of America. Today, because of the addition of several male members, the guild is called the Daughters of Dorcas and Sons.

Like the biblical character Dorcas, who applied her sewing skills to the needs of her community, Mrs. Canady freely gives of her time, energy, and wisdom to all who seek her. She has dedicated herself to preserving the art of quilting for African Americans. To this end, she has taught quiltmaking to children at several places, including the Sumner School Museum in Washington, D.C. Although she enjoys a national reputation for her stained-glass appliqué, Mrs. Canady teaches piecing precise geometric patterns. One of her favorite quilts is her Pieced Star Quilt, a multicolored, vibrant quilt in which bold color combinations work well within a given geometric frame. This seemingly simple yet eloquent quilt is indicative of a long-standing African American custom that goes back as far as the time of slavery. That custom is to place bold, colorful fabric within a precise structured pattern.

Mrs. Canady is a master seamstress and quilter. She began her apprenticeship as a child helping her mother and grandmother piece quilt tops to sell to white women. She explains how her mother and other African American women would piece perfect geometric patterns for white women who would exhibit the quilts as their own creations. Mrs. Canady's story is not unusual. Many geometric-patterned quilts made by African American women, both slave and free, are now white families' heirlooms. To identify these quilts today would be difficult at best. And yet they are truly African American quilts.

One all too common story within the African American community regarding old quilts is that of discarded utilitarian and even some geometric quilts. The very quilts that might have served to map paths to freedom have received the harshest of treatment and have been the most devalued and badly neglected within the African American community. All too often these quilts have been discarded. In *A Howard Reader: An Intellectual and Cultural Quilt of the African American Experience*, Raymond writes:

The African American quilt is all too often dismissed as something old, tattered, discolored and "in pieces." We often fail to
look deeper—fail to realize that which is old and torn is spiritually textured; that which is stained is marked by grace; and that
which is fragmented comes together to create something new,
whole and beautiful. The quilt can be a visual metaphor for per-
severance and continuity. The many scraps of fabric needed to
make a quilt similar to "A Pieced Star" usually have special
meaning because they are taken from garments of deceased relatives or given as tokens of friendship. The quilt then becomes
a visible and tangible link to the past and a connection to the fu-
ture. . . . (p. xii)

Contemporary African American quilter Elizabeth Scott perhaps
best exemplifies the continuation of the narrative tradition of her
African ancestors, weaving her stories in textiles and encoding her
memories on fabric in appliquéd symbols, enclosed objects, and stitching. Within her repository of quilts and fabric art, Scott brings together most of the African textile traditions we have discussed.
Whether executed by conscious choice or by a "model in the mind,"
Scott's work stands as testament to her cultural heritage and the storytelling tradition.

Scott's Plantation Quilt (see color photo section) clearly emerges
from the African tradition of appliqué as seen in the Fon of Dahomey.
With its cluster of stars boldly dotting the fabric landscape, giving the
viewer a window from her eyes heavenward on a night as seen from her
South Carolina porch, we see what she sees. We are at once reminded
of the star mapping techniques of the Pawnee as well as the Bible
quilts of Harriet Powers with their star-studded blocks. What is most
interesting about this quilt, however, is the stitching. The hand stitch-

ing on this quilt forms a topographical map in patches, as if one were standing on one of the stars and looking down from the heavens. Scott gives us a double perspective. We are at the same time looking up at the heavens and down at the earth, and both are connected in this "story" she reveals to us. Reminiscent of Sweet Clara stitching a topographical map onto her quilt, Elizabeth Scott has created mapping for both a heavenly journey, perhaps to "follow the stars," as well as a geographic map, perhaps to lead us off the plantation and on to the "crossroads" and freedom.

In her quilt *Rocks in Prison*, Scott tells her story in a more abstract or "encoded" form than she did in her Plantation Quilt. Scott regards the rocks seen lined in a rectangular grid in the center of the piece as remembrances of the chain gangs who had to "bust" the rocks. She connects this in her own mind and on the quilt with a biblical reference to "in the beginning," when rocks came before man. In each corner of this quilt Scott has embedded a rock, perhaps evoking the symbols of the Kongo cosmogram and the four moments of the sun, as well as the cycle of birth, life, death, and rebirth. It is the knowledge of American and African traditions that allows us to interpret Mrs. Scott's quilts on so many levels.

Rocks are used in a more deliberate and utilitarian manner in her shawl entitled *Prayer*. In this piece Scott has drawn on her belief in the healing power of the rocks to aid with her arthritis and other illnesses. Used in this way, the rocks act as *minkisi*, or charms, that have been created for healing. We have seen this belief in the power and symbolism of rocks used by the Sande women's secret society of West Africa. Is Mrs. Scott carrying on a women's tradition known by her ancestors?

Another Time is a tactile piece creating its rich texture through the extensive use of buttons and beads. Through touch and sight, the observer is witness to a modern-day *lukasa* memory board created on fabric. In this case, as in the case of the Luba *lukasa*, the meaning lies hidden to those who cannot read the symbols.

We liken Mrs. Elizabeth Scott to a "fabric griot," one who preserves and passes on the stories of her family and her ancestors. It is, again, our responsibility to see, listen, and pass on the stories of our elders, whether those stories are found in the quilts in the attic, heard at Grandpa's knee, or seen in the art of our contemporaries. The stories are there; it remains for us to claim them.

Epilogue

by Jacqueline Tobin

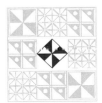

THE STORY OF QUILTS AND THE UNDERGROUND RAILROAD HAS enveloped my life for over five years now. Ozella's gift of story has taken me places geographically and intellectually I could not even have dreamed of that day of our initial meeting in the Charleston Marketplace. My search for the origins and context for this book placed me in the company of an exciting cast of people: African American scholars, Sea Island basketmakers, Gullah storytellers, African textile specialists, low-country agriculturalists, historical preservationists, some of the last African American craftspersons carrying on their ancestral traditions, and Mississippi Delta story quilters.

During this time I walked remote and diminishing South Carolina and Georgia coastlines; I sat for days amid pails of sweet grass and palmetto, rode a horse-drawn carriage past architectural remnants of

King Cotton, rice, and indigo, and strode along rows of slave cabins hidden away from the Big House. I stood where Africans landed in captivity and looked across the Atlantic as they did, envisioning their African homeland and the portals of slavery. I walked the hallowed grounds of Civil War battlefields and crossed the fields where Blue met Gray. I sat in slave-crafted pews inscribed with tribal signatures and looked down at floorboards bored with holes for those hiding underneath. I toured Fort Sumter, where the slave-hewed brick walls stand as testimony to those whose freedom these walls signified.

When I was still, I could hear the haunting sounds of spirituals, their words encoding freedom, and the tapping of feet drumming out messages of hope. I have learned from the bush schools of the Sande and had secrets revealed to me by descendants of the original Prince Hall Masons. I arrived, at last, when I was ready, in Buxton Township, Ontario, and freedom's door. I was invited in by the descendants of those who had followed the North Star. Everywhere, the ancestors guided me. I felt their presence in everyone I met.

I have been privileged by the gift of Ozella's story and by her guiding words. While she was intent on passing on the story, as her mother and grandmother had before her, I also became intrigued by Ozella herself. I discovered through relatives that Ozella was a college graduate and that she had attended graduate school at Howard University. I heard about her retirement from teaching school in California and her return to Charleston to become both the "lemonade lady" and the "Marketplace quilter." She was indeed an anomaly, even to her relatives. Ozella wanted the attention to be on the story rather than on herself. I followed her words where they led me, always in pursuit of truth.

But there remained one last task: a return to the griot, my mentor, Ozella McDaniel Williams of Charleston, South Carolina. I did not know why I was returning again, only that I knew I had to.

I was saddened to find that Ozella no longer went to the Marketplace to sell her quilts. Her health prevented her from sitting in the outdoor arena where I first approached her. So our meeting took place, not amid the hustle and bustle of the Charleston Marketplace as before, but in the living room of the home Ozella now shared with her older brother. But even here, in the confines of her living room, Ozella still sat amid piles and piles and rows of her handmade quilts.

When I reached Ozella's home, she was dressed as before in her hand-painted white hat and blouse. Her face and body, once animated and lively, now reflected a tiredness earned through a lifetime of work.

Once again, Ozella instructed me to sit down. Her elder brother sat with us. He was dressed in overalls and straw hat, both hands cradling a cane. He was voiceless during our visit, but every now and then, in response to some statement, he would nod in agreement and smile knowingly. There was always a twinkle in his eye while Ozella spoke. He became a silent participant in our conversation. Ozella said, "He knows something but won't ever talk. My mother told all of us the story, but I was the only one who paid any attention. We lived on land in Callison, South Carolina, in McCormick County. We would all sit underneath a large oak tree at night and our parents would tell us stories. This is where my mother and grandmother would show us how to quilt. Holding up a particular quilt pattern, my grandmother or mother would instruct us in the sewing of it and also tell us how that particular pattern was placed inside of the story I told you."

The aura of teacher and student, griot and initiate, still surrounded us, but the atmosphere had changed. Ozella had not changed; I had been changed. Knowing now that I had indeed been chosen to pass the story on and preserve it for history, I felt a deep sense of humility, gratitude, and indebtedness.

I knew that Ozella had no children to pass the story on to. Raymond and I had also discovered that although she had attempted to tell her story to others, no one had demonstrated any interest. Moreover, Ozella's nephew had stated emphatically that his aunt "never told the whole story to anyone at one time." Was I the only person to really persist in getting the story? Was I the only one who paid attention when she spoke? Was I the child entrusted to keep the family stories?

Ozella had taken the tradition of the African griot to a level where, like the realm of the spirit, there is no separation by race. In telling me the story, Ozella moved beyond the strictures of the past. Wading in the ancestral stream, I knew Ozella was preparing me to be a griot as well. My lessons had begun with the words "Write this down."

Tonight she continued to prepare me. Calling me "little girl" in a tone of admonishment, she instructed me to go home and stand in front of a large mirror and have my husband or sister or someone else hurl insulting barbs at me. She told me to watch myself and see if I could withstand the insults without visibly flinching. She was checking my mental posture, ensuring that I was prepared to stand in the shoes of a people who bore every kind of indignity but were not broken. She was preparing me to stand in the presence of the ancestors and tell their story.

After further conversation, I stood at last to go. I moved toward Ozella and reverently placed a silver necklace around her neck. She looked down at the necklace, studying the symbol it held, then looked up at me with a smile on her face.

"Among the Native peoples of the Southwest pueblos there is a symbol, as on this necklace, that represents the storyteller," I told her. "The seated figure, a man or woman surrounded by children, represents that person in Native cultures who passes on the stories of that people. In your culture, Ozella, these persons are known as griots. You are that person."

Her eyes slowly moved from the storyteller necklace to myself. For a moment lasting forever, our eyes met. Through the eyes of recognition and acknowledgment, amid the pile of quilts, we honored both the story and the storyteller.

I left her home reluctantly. As I entered the awaiting cab I turned for one last look. Ozella was standing there, her body framed by the door and lit from within. One hand was holding the door; the other, tightly closed on her chest, held the storyteller necklace.

Ozella McDaniel Williams passed away in Charleston, South Carolina, on May 17, 1998, two weeks after I had last seen and talked with her. In the "home-going services" held for her on May 23, Ozella was laid to rest with the song "May the Work I've Done Speak for Me."

While on the Journey to Canaan: Survival Secrets

by Raymond G. Dobard and Jacqueline L. Tobin

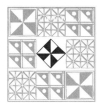

THE LATE OZELLA MCDANIEL WILLIAMS OF CHARLESTON, South Carolina, an African American storyteller in the tradition of the African griot, or keeper of stories, opened a door onto the past and revealed to the world a story of racial transcendence. What was kept behind closed doors, enshrined in a historic market stall filled with quilts, and reserved for the ears of only chosen family members, was given to the world when Ozella instructed Jacqueline Tobin in 1996 to "Write this down." The secret quilt code used by Ozella's ancestors to assist fellow enslaved blacks in their escape to freedom became the subject of *Hidden in Plain View*.

Now, for the first time, the story continues with the second part of the code that Ozella revealed first to Jacqueline Tobin in 1996 and repeated in story form to both authors in 1997. This "secondary code," also "hidden" in the language of quilt patterns, tells the story of what the fleeing slaves had to do in order to survive while on their perilous journey North toward Canada. We begin by citing the secondary code here in Ozella's words:

Ladies tied their heads up in sunbonnets and bandannas and went out gardening in nine different patches by the moonlight. Men put on coveralls and went fishing on sailboats and came back and ate fish on the Dresden plates.

Anyone died on the way they would weave baskets and leave at the cemetery. And they would take muscadine vines and they would pick wild flowers and make wreaths and also leave at the cemetery.

Let us go now to a scene that takes place at night on the docks of nineteenth-century Cleveland, Ohio, Ozella's acclaimed crossroads, where secrecy is supreme and chaos choreographs the actions of longshoremen, sailors, dock workers, well-wishers, and passengers waiting to board. Some of these anxiously awaiting passengers are fugitives in disguise. They must endure one last encounter with danger, perhaps the most perilous and challenging part of their journey to freedom.

The sounds of creaking wood and lapping water accompany a chorus of voices giving directions and expressing good-byes. All activity is carefully monitored by the ever-present slave catchers who plague the docks, knowing that this is their last chance to capture runaway slaves. The night air is charged with fear, desperation, hope, and determined courage. Moonlight competes with the flickering glare of torches and distorted shadows. Boats patiently wait to receive their precious cargo and to ferry them to the new land of Canaan, to Ontario, Canada.

At the same time, the docks of other port cities set the stage for similar scenes of danger and promise. For example, Sandusky, a city about forty-one miles to the west of Cleveland, was another very important freedom port, as explained by Wilbur Siebert, the respected nineteenth-century author of *The Underground Railroad: From Slavery to Freedom.* Sandusky, according to Siebert, was home to a large number of prosperous free blacks who would have been able to assist fleeing bondsmen and -women. In addition to Cleveland and Sandusky, the port city of Detroit, Michigan, was also pivotal to the freedom movement, according to numerous documents. Detroit's serendipitous location and geography enabled many to cross into Ontario, Canada, at Windsor, where Lake Erie narrows to a mere river.

The first half of Ozella's Code allowed us to trace one possible route of escape, from the low country of South Carolina through the Appalachian Mountains, into Ohio, to Cleveland and beyond. If the first portion of the code identified a possible route of escape, the second part of the code addressed the needs of the fugitives along the journey. Primary among these needs, as Ozella put it, was a kind of personal emancipation: the fugitives had to break their mental chains as well as their physical bondage. Yes, the fugitives needed to put on new clothes and use external disguises; however, they had to also change inside if they were to walk boldly past the scrutinizing stares of slave catchers and onto the boats docked along Lake Erie. Freedom demanded an internal as well as external change.

What does the second half of Ozella's Code tell us about this transformation? A fugitive's disguise had to go beyond surface costumes to the very essence of self-identity. Disguises were common on the Underground Railroad. Underground Railroad history is replete with published firsthand accounts and orally transmitted stories detailing how disguises helped fugitives to freedom. From Harriet Tubman, who dressed as a man or wore a bonnet to hide her face, to Frederick Douglass, who dressed as a black sailor, or "Black Jack," with red bandanna, blue boater, and forged papers, to Ellen Craft, who was so fair that she could disguise herself as a white man with her husband posing as her slave, disguise was critical for many fugitives. In the first part of Ozella's Code, the quilt pattern known as "Cotton and Satin Bow Ties" symbolized a disguise of fancy clothes. The second part of the code refers to sunbonnets, bandannas, and coveralls. What might these clothes mean to a fugitive's survival?

As we discussed in *Hidden in Plain View*, sunbonnets and bandannas were indicators of social rank. The bonnets of the Quakers and other women of the nineteenth century helped to cover their faces from the harsh rays of the sun as well as provide an element of modesty. The dresses of Quaker women were plain yet elegant, the contrast to the embellished satin clothing of wealthy women, since the Quakers' religious custom frowned upon a pious woman wearing brightly colored clothes. We know that Harriet Tubman used bonnets to disguise herself, and wide-brimmed sunbonnets would have been particularly useful as a disguise for slave women of light complexion. What then can we make of the bandannas?

Plain, scalp-fitting kerchiefs were often proscribed by law for black female servants, most notably in New Orleans but in other areas of the South as well. "Bandannas" may also refer to the Tignon (or Chignon), an elaborate headdress worn by free black women as an indication of their status in a community. The Tignon is African in origin and could be fashioned from fancy cloth or silk. It is a sign of pride, and the precursor to the elaborate hats black women wear to this day when attending Sunday church services or other special community celebrations.

A fair-skinned female fugitive might wear a bonnet and be accompanied by a dark-skinned female fugitive wearing a simple bandanna, giving the impression of a white woman with her servant. They would then be able to walk past the slave catchers and board the ships headed for Canada, provided that the fair-skinned woman convincingly assumed the bearing of a white woman, and the dark-skinned woman appeared comfortable in her role as servant. The black women wearing the more elaborate African-style bandannas or Tignons could hold their heads up high and walk confidently past the slave catchers, defying them to ask for their manumission papers.

What is the meaning of gardening in the moonlight? Why the reference to nine gardening patches, and why the number nine in particular? The Nine Patch is the name of a favorite quilt pattern in which three rows of three squares, nine squares in total, form a cross within a square. Might nine be the number of safe havens or other port locations to which the fugitives would be taken? Or nine may refer to the number of days, weeks, or months needed to complete the breaking of mental chains, to impart new skills, new trades needed to obtain employment in cities where industrialization and skill in brick masonry, carpentry, and other trades superceded farming. Or the "nine *different* patches" may refer to topography, to the landscape as seen on the quilt of Sweet Clara in Deborah Hopkinson's *Sweet Clara and the Freedom Quilt*, or the furrow-like stitches in Elizabeth Scott's 1981 *Plantation Quilt*. As unusual as this combination of elements appears, there is rhyme, reason, and logic here. Moonlight might also indicate a time of day or possibly a particular place. For example, Detroit was called "Midnight" in the Alexander Ross Code.

The docks, with the freedom fleet awaiting, must have pulsed with the anxiety of so many passengers hoping for a safe and trouble-free boarding. The most probable time that these special boardings occurred was in the dark of night, when unsteady street lamps and torches cast flickering lights and distorted shadows on all. Only after the boats departed and were a distance from the shore would the peaceful, clear moonlight extinguish the harsh glare of probing torches. Black and white sailors would soon be joined in steering the ships by some of the male fugitives now able to physically help in their own escape. Remember that fugitives escaping from the low country of South Carolina would often have been skillful sailors in their own right. Many would have learned their skills in the rivers of West Africa; others would attain their training as they moved down the rivers and waterways along the coastal islands that dot the South Carolina and Georgia coastlines.

The second part of Ozella's Quilt Code tells us that the men went fishing on sailboats wearing overalls. The overalls, the uniform of long-shoremen and deckhands, enabled male fugitives to walk in the company of regular sailors, longshoremen, and dock workers, many of whom were black. The male fugitives learned the language and mannerisms of dock workers. Many probably became sailors and could then board the boats without suspicion. They were most likely provided with forged papers identifying them as free black sailors; remember Frederick Douglass, for example. Douglass and numerous other male slaves, hired out by their masters to work on the dock or even on ships, made valuable contacts with free black sailors and sympathetic white seamen, who taught the enslaved men all they needed to know about sailing.

The Code continues, "they caught fish and returned to eat the fish on Dresden plates." Dresden plates does not mean the fine porcelain of Meissen, Germany. Nor does the reference identify the famous quilt pattern of twentieth-century America. What did Dresden plates mean? We already know of Dresden, Ohio, and its importance to the Underground Railroad. But this Dresden, if a city, must be beyond the journey's "crossroads" of Cleveland: and indeed it was.

Just a few miles to the northeast of Windsor, Ontario, were the settlements of Buxton and Chatham, both hubs for Underground Railroad strategy sessions attended by such notable abolitionists as Harriet Tubman, Frederick Douglass, and John Brown. Buxton, Ontario, was one of several sites where planned settlements for newly escaping bondsmen were located; other sites included the nearby Dawn and Elgin

Settlements. Close by in this region of safe havens, and overlapping the Dawn Settlement, was the city of Dresden, Ontario: a city alluded to in Ozella's Code. These settlements were founded by both white and free black people of good will, including the famous former slave Josiah Henson, who inspired the character of Uncle Tom in Harriet Beecher Stowe's novel.

Fugitives were able to sail directly from Cleveland to the Dresden area via Windsor, Ontario, or Detroit, Michigan: from Cleveland, Dresden was reachable by sailing directly to Windsor and then on small craft or by land to Dresden. An alternative was to sail to Detroit, Michigan, and then cross over into Windsor, Canada. The Code's reference to Dresden may be a clever allusion, a trip from one Dresden to another—Ohio to Ontario.

Dresden, Ontario is a city with a very rich history and with multiple ties to the Underground Railroad. Josiah Henson's name is synonymous with the Dawn settlement, a settlement of fugitive slaves that later became a part of Dresden. In 1842, Josiah Henson, with the help of like-minded friends, founded the Dawn Institute right next to Dresden as a refuge and a training center for fugitive slaves. In addition, Henson was an ordained pastor of the British Methodist Church in Dresden. The British Methodist Church belonged to the African Episcopal Methodist Church, an organization that participated in Underground Railroad activities. Josiah Henson was also a member of the Mount Moriah Lodge #4, a Prince Hall Masonic Lodge in Dresden, where he served as secretary.

In addition to the Josiah Henson connection, Dresden might well be a part of the Alexander Ross Code. Alexander Ross, a Canadian ornithologist, devised a code using numbers, poetic descriptions, and pious praises. Recorded in Henrietta Buckmaster's *Flight to Freedom: The Story of the Underground Railroad*, the Ross Code reads as follows:

Pennsylvania was called number 10; Seville, Ohio was number
20; Medina, Ohio was number 27; Cleveland, Ohio was named
"Hope"; Sandusky, Ohio was known as "Sunrise" and Detroit,
Michigan was labeled "Midnight." The entry ports into Canada
were identified by praises to God: "Glory to God" signaled
Windsor, Ontario, and "God be praised" hailed Port Stanley,
Ontario. Ross referred to his passengers as "packages:" males
were "hardware" and females were "dry goods." (p. 249)

A proposed message might read: *Expect two packages of hardware and
three of dry goods. We hope to send them by sunrise so that they might arrive at
midnight, Glory to God, and opened before dawn.* Translated, the message
says: "Expect two male and three female fugitives. They will travel from
Cleveland via Sandusky, Detroit, and Windsor to Dresden." The connection from Cleveland to Sandusky to Detroit to Dresden is a logical
one. To travel from Detroit to Dresden would then be to go from
"Midnight" to "Dawn."

Since Cleveland was a port city and home to many ships, there existed
many routes on Lake Erie. Perhaps the nine "garden patches" referred to
these routes as well as to ship lines. The prudent thing would have been
for the fugitive party to break up and "garden," to break new ground by
traveling along unexpected routes. There were enough sea captains and
boats of varying sizes to accommodate a large number of people. After
all, to travel as one large party would attract attention.

The last line of the second part of the Code seems to be discussing a
cemetery and whatever burial rites were available to those who did not survive the journey. *Anyone died on their way they would weave baskets and leave
at the cemetery. And they take muscadine vines and they would pick wild flowers
and make wreaths and also leave at the cemetery.*

Here we are confronted with another paradox. The Code surely does not imply that fleeing slaves would take the time to actually weave baskets to leave at a cemetery. Should a fugitive die on the journey North, that fugitive would have to be buried in an unmarked grave in order to protect the others from detection. To raise a small mound of earth or to place a marker of any kind would attract attention and give away the trail. Slave catchers were sure to follow. The burial place had to be indistinguishable from the rest of the woodland. For the final time, something special would have to have been hidden in plain view.

The African American custom of marking graves with shells, broken dishes, stones, tools, cooking utensils, pinwheels, and even quilts in honor of the deceased was a luxury the fleeing fugitives could not afford. What then does the final phrase mean? If we interpret this final portion of the Code symbolically, the references to death most likely address some indicators, some signs that danger lay ahead and that it was necessary for the fugitive party to take a detour.

We know that there are many Indian grave mounds in Ohio within the crossing area between Wheeling, West Virginia, and Marietta, Ohio. Prior to their destruction in the early twentieth century, several mounds once punctuated the landscape just outside of Dresden, Ohio, according to Leland Beers, the authority on Dresden and the author of *Towpath Topsy*. In addition, muscadine grape vineyards, which are also in abundance in South Carolina, grace Ohio along the bluffs near Lake Erie because of conducive climatic conditions. Some vineyards are also found to the south of Sandusky. Given these geographic considerations, the Code passage signals to stop and take an alternate route past the grave mounds and through the vineyards to a port city other than Cleveland. Sandusky is a strong possibility.

Does this explain the reason why when an object cannot be found in an African American house, or when something disappears, elders often will say "I guess that's gone by way of Sandusky?" Was to "go by way of

Sandusky" to vanish within the free black community for training, for employment, and the chance to make money in preparation for their relocation in Canada? Was "by way of Sandusky" an indication to take the long way around to some destination (a suggestion of researcher-historian Joan Beaubian of New Bedford, Massachusetts)? Did "by way of Sandusky" mean to hide?

Like the signal to travel in a zigzag pattern deduced from the first part of Ozella's Code, the "weaving of baskets" might well have directed the fugitives to weave their way in and out, skipping some houses as they traveled toward the alternate destination. Another interpretation for this final section of the secondary code involves actual cemeteries located between the eastern Ohio border region of Marietta-Wheeling and the Cleveland-Sandusky area. Perhaps the fugitive party moved from cemetery to cemetery, taking refuge there until receiving an all-clear signal. The signal may have been a quilt with the Pin Wheel pattern placed on a grave: in discussions of this part of the Code, Ozella often talked about the use of pinwheels as a means of determining when and where to travel. After determining the direction of the wind, the escaping slaves could discern the best direction to travel forward so as not to allow their scents to be discovered by searching bloodhounds.

Objects left on graves in a cemetery might not necessarily draw attention. After all, it was not unusual for grieving relatives to leave favored objects of the deceased on top of the grave, especially if the grave was that of a child. Might a basket of wildflowers resting on a particular grave indicate that the fugitives were to travel to a nearby meadow, a place where wildflowers grew in abundance? Might the reference to the muscadine vine wreath be a directive to a vineyard where muscadine grapes grew? Were the fugitives to travel from the foothills of the Appalachians to an ancient grave mound of the Native Americans or a graveyard, and move from there to a meadow and finally to the vineyards adjacent to a city?

What about the many wreaths engraved on cemetery stones or the equally common graveyard sculptures of women holding wreaths? The engraved stone wreaths stand out among the graveyard decorations, and the stone wreaths held aloft by the female figures are also prominent. These highly visible figures, personifications of the seasons of the year, intimate the passage of time and may well have been signposts. We have two possible signs here: one a vineyard, the other a graveyard. And what about the baskets?

We know that baskets were the everyday containers African American women carried, especially in the sweet-grass lowlands of South Carolina. Baskets without bottoms were placed on graves as containers that left spirits free to move on and not be held. Ozella's reference may indicate particular baskets left on a grave in a specific cemetery, as a place to receive and leave messages.

Although this "secondary" portion of the code is left to further interpretation, the one concrete link it made for us was to Dresden, Ontario. Might these many possible images constitute a trail directing the fugitives to an alternate one? This last portion of Ozella's Code is enigmatic at best. In keeping with African Secret Society traditions, with the obvious layering of meaning throughout the entire code, and with Ozella's own intentions to not reveal anything all at one time; perhaps we are now left to ponder and accept Ozella's original words and realize that "you will get the story when you are ready." It is with honor and respect that we submit this secondary code and await further revelations.

Timeline

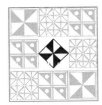

15th century	Slavery, dating back to antiquity, comes under European control due to economic expansion westward
1440	First large-scale enslavement of African peoples by western Europeans
16th–19th centuries	Transatlantic slave trade disperses millions of slaves to European colonies in the New World
1619	First Africans arrive in Jamestown, Virginia, initially identified as indentured servants

1641	Massachusetts Bay Colony sanctions enslavement of African workers; status of white indentured servants remains the same
1660	Maryland and Virginia legalize slavery of Africans; status of children to be determined by status of the mother
1739	Stono Rebellion; South Carolina Sea Island slaves rebel and attempt to reach Florida; over one hundred killed
1745–97	Olaudah Equiano; former slave who wrote his autobiography, entitled *Life*, totally by himself, thus dispelling myth that blacks could not represent themselves by themselves
1753–84	Phillis Wheatley; former slave; first African American to publish a book; most noted for her poetry about being Negro, a former slave, and a woman
1755	All thirteen colonies legally recognize chattel slavery
1770s	Slave labor becomes vital to Southern economy due to plantations system of growing rice, tobacco, sugarcane, and indigo; Northern economy grows toward development of small farms and industry
1775	Prince Hall and fourteen other free blacks initiated into British Army Lodge Masonic Order, stationed at Boston Harbor, first African American Masonic Order

1776	Declaration of Independence signed
1786	One of earliest organized slave escapes documented when Quakers aid runaways from Virginia
1787	U.S. Constitution drafted; forbids Congress from interfering with slave trade before 1808; enslaved persons counted as three-fifths of a person in census
1787	Prince Hall receives charter for African Lodge No. 1; African Masonic Lodges later named after their founder, Prince Hall
1793	Invention of cotton gin ensures importance of slavery to Southern economy
1793	Canada's only antislavery law passed
1793	First Fugitive Slave Law passed
1801	First Caucasian Masonic Lodge established in Charleston, South Carolina
1803	Haiti achieves independence from France; abolishes slavery
1816	British abandon Fort Gadson in Florida; Seminole Indians and fugitive slaves take it over and rename it Fort Negro; Andrew Jackson is dispensed by the government to take it again, thus beginning the Seminole Wars

1817	Andrew Jackson takes command of federal troops engaging in war against Seminoles and African American runaways in Florida
1822	Denmark Vesey, a free black in Charleston, organizes plan to free slaves; he is betrayed by a slave who told his master about the plot; Vesey and thirty-four slaves are executed
1822	Eighteen slaves from the Ibo tribe link arms and wade into Dunbar Creek saying, "Water brought us and water's gonna take us away." Site now called Ibo Landing, located on St. Simons Island, Georgia; their actions are now celebrated in Negro spiritual, "Oh, Freedom"
1829	David Walker publishes his "Appeal," which is smuggled aboard ships heading to the South and passed around Southern cities; in it Walker calls for violent resistance to slavery
1829	Isabella Van Wagener changes her name to Sojourner Truth, becomes an abolitionist, and starts preaching in the North
1830s	Rise in popularity of the railroad train lends name and image to movement of escaping slaves
1831	Nat Turner, slave and preacher, leads seventy-five slaves in revolt to take Virginia armory; he is later captured and killed
1831	William Lloyd Garrison begins publication of abolitionist newspaper *The Liberator*

1833	British Emancipation Act; all slavery abolished in British Empire, including Canada
1838	Black abolitionist Robert Purvis becomes chairman of the General Vigilance Committee in New York; purpose is to assist runaways
1839	Spanish ship *Amistad* taken over by illegally enslaved Africans who mutinied; trying to return to Africa, they end up off Long Island coast; Spaniards go to court to get Africans back; enslaved Africans were members of Mende Poro secret society; John Quincy Adams defends Africans before the Supreme Court, who ruled in 1840 that a slave who escapes illegal bondage is free; *Amistad* Africans return to Africa
1839-1911	Harriet Powers; sewed her Bible quilts (Smithsonian Quilt dates to 1886, Boston Fine Arts Quilt around 1895)
1847	First Prince Hall Masonic Lodge established in Hamilton, Ontario
1847-63	Frederick Douglass, U.S. abolitionist and escaped slave, publishes newspaper, the *North Star*
1848	First Women's Rights Convention held in Seneca Falls, New York; abolitionists Lucretia Mott, Elizabeth Cady Stanton, and Frederick Douglass attend; women's rights and abolitionist movements join forces

1849	Harriet Tubman, escaped slave, leads over three hundred slaves to freedom via Underground Railroad over a period of several years
1850	Second Fugitive Slave Law passed
1851	Harriet Beecher Stowe publishes *Uncle Tom's Cabin*, which reveals the harshness of slavery and stimulates abolitionist sentiments
1851	Sojourner Truth gives "Ain't I a Woman" speech at women's rights convention in Akron, Ohio, protesting both racial and gender stereotyping
1856	Henry "Box" Brown mails himself in wooden crate from Richmond, Virginia, to Philadelphia to the Anti-Slavery Society to attain freedom; he succeeds
1857	Dred Scott Case; Supreme Court rules against Dred Scott, who filed suit claiming freedom when his owner took him to the free state of Illinois but then sent Scott back to Missouri, a slave state
1858	On Jekyll Island, Georgia, slave ship *Wanderer* arrives carrying what may have been the last cargo of slaves to America
1859	John Brown, U.S. abolitionist, raids arsenal at Harper's Ferry to attain guns to lead slave insurrection; captured and hanged later that year
1861	Outbreak of Civil War with the firing on Fort Sumter, South Carolina

1862	Penn School on St. Helena Island, South Carolina, founded; one of the first Southern schools for newly freed slaves; Laura Towne and Ellen Murray were founders; Charlotte Forten became the first black teacher in 1863
1863	Abraham Lincoln issues Emancipation Proclamation
1863	African American Masonic members compose 54th Massachusetts Brigade stationed in Charleston, South Carolina, across the street from the Citadel
1865	End of Civil War with the surrender of Confederate forces
1865	Thirteenth amendment to Constitution prohibits slavery in United States
1872	William Still, free black in Philadelphia and most famous conductor, writes his book *The Underground Railroad*; he interviewed every runaway sent to him and chronicled their stories in this book
1898	Wilbur Siebert publishes *The Underground Railroad: From Slavery to Freedom*

Ozella's Underground Railroad Quilt Code Patterns

Monkey Wrench

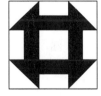

Wagon Wheel/
Carpenter's Wheel

Wagon Wheel Variation

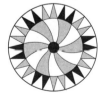

Bear's Paw

Crossroads

Log Cabin

Shoofly

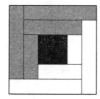

Bow Tie (also known
as Hourglass)

Flying Geese

Drunkard's Path

Star/Evening Star/
North Star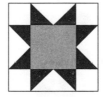

Tumbling Blocks
or Boxes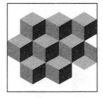

OZELLA'S SECONDARY "CODE" PATTERNS

Sailboat

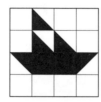

Britches

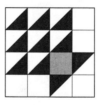

Basket

Nine Patch

Rose Wreath

Broken Dishes

Chart Comparing African Symbols, American Quilt Patterns, and Masonic Emblems

African Symbols	American Quilt Patterns	Masonic Emblems
Hausa: *Five Houses* (pattern found on embroidered menswear as part of the eight knives design)	*Nine Patch* *Basic Unit*	*Checkerboard* (the tile floor of the lodge bears the pattern)
Poro Secret Society *Two Double Pyramids*	*Hourglass or Bow Tie*	*Hourglass*
Aiyasa Secret Society *Two Superimposed Pyramids*	*Double X Pattern*	*The Square and Compass*
Egbo Secret Society *Five-Pointed Star*	*Five-Pointed Star*	*Five-Pointed Star and Eastern Star*

African Symbols	American Quilt Patterns	Masonic Emblems

Bakongo and Epke
Leopard Society
(mirror reflection of
Broken Dishes pattern)

Broken Dishes

No equivalent.

*Repeated
Hourglass and Bow Tie*
(pattern forming a block)

*Pinwheel Hidden in
Hourglass and Bow Tie*

No equivalent.

Epke Cloth
of the Leopard Society
(repeated right triangles
forming a patterned block)

*Birds in the Air and
Flock of Geese*

No equivalent.

Glossary

✤ ACHE   Life force pulsating through the body when participating in African dances.

✤ ADINKRA CLOTH   Made by Asante people of Ghana out of cotton cloth. Stamps derived from secret society scripts are dipped in black bark dye and pressed onto the cloth, creating patterns.

✤ ADIRE CLOTH   Made by Yoruba people of Nigeria, using resist dye method with indigo-blue dye on one side of cloth, creating blue-on-blue patterns.

✤ APPLIQUÉ   To appliqué a design or figurative motif is to apply an image directly to the top of a fabric block. With the exception of the blind stitch, all other stitches show and are incorporated into the general design. The broderie perse, running stitch, and blanket stitch are the most common used.

❖ BACKING   The quilt backing serves to stabilize the entire quilt and enables the quilter to enclose the batting. When possible, the backing is composed of one solid seamless sheet of fabric. Because fabric widths ranged between the twenty-three and thirty-six inches during the eighteenth and nineteenth centuries and today's fabric measures forty-two inches, seams are to be expected. In fact, these seams and the backing fabric widths aid in dating the quilts.

❖ BAMBOULA   African dance named for Bamboula talking drum; seen as early form of tap dancing.

❖ BATTING   The quilt batting is the center portion of the "quilt sandwich." Combed cotton, whether in high or low loft, is the most common material chosen. Cotton batting is usually thin (low loft) and affords the quilter the opportunity to make small regular stitches. These stitches can be as small as twelve or more stitches per inch. If the batting is made of old clothing or any heavy insulating material, the stitches will be larger. These stitches do not indicate an aesthetic preference, but are the result of practicality. It is impossible to make small stitches through thick or coarse batting material using the traditional rocking method of quilting. To make small stitches through heavy batting would require the quilter to make one stitch at a time, piercing the quilt sandwich from the top down through the batting and then blindly from the bottom back up. When the batting is an old discarded quilt (the quilt within a quilt), an old worn blanket, or remnants of old clothing, the method of binding the layers together is called tacking or tying, using twine, cord, or yarn. This method produces ties on the quilt top that are knotted. Usually two knots are sufficient (unlike the Underground Railroad Quilt Code quilts, where five square knots appeared).

❖ BOGOLANFINI CLOTH   Made from white cotton strips handwoven by men and then dyed by women using mud-based dye. The ideographs and geometric designs created on the cloth form a code writing system. The designs are passed down from generation to generation.

❖ CABLE TOW   A length of knotted rope used by initiates in Masonic orders; rope serves as tie and measurement and holds special meaning.

❖ CALL AND RESPONSE   African musical technique used to evoke participation of the audience by responding verbally, by clapping, and/or by foot-stomping.

❖ EASTERN STAR   Women's division of Masonic organization.

❖ FELLOWCRAFT   Masonic initiate.

❖ FON   People of Republic of Benin (formerly Dahomey) known for appliquéd textiles that tell stories; seen as inspiration for storytelling quilts in African American tradition.

❖ GRIOT   African term for community storyteller and keeper of cultural heritage, history, and stories.

❖ HAUSA   Nigerian West African people known for their embroidered designs; some designs distinctly Islamic in character (H. E. Kiewe);

others create geographical map; designs are guarded from one generation to another.

✥ KONGO COSMOGRAM   The cosmogram represents the four moments of the sun, a reference to the cycles of life. An X or cross inscribed on textiles, art, and ground drawings, representing sacred place where oaths could be taken; cross represents separation of world of the living and world of the dead or ancestors; often described as "crossroads."

✥ KUBA RAFFIA CLOTH   Central Kongo textile design noted for appliquéd shapes, which some scholars think are symbolic and hold secret meaning.

✥ LUKASA   In Luba culture in southeastern Kongo, a flat, hand-sized wooden rectangular or hourglass-shaped object studded with beads, pins, and covered with inscribed symbols. The *lukasa* is a memory device; beads constitute a kind of alphabet; *lukasa* has come to generically mean any object or word used to stir memory.

✥ MANDE   Both a broad-based culture and a language. As a language, Mande belongs to the Niger-Congo family of languages spoken in places such as Mali, Guinea, the Ivory Coast, Liberia, and Sierra Leone.

✥ MENDE   A people who live in southern Sierra Leone and eastern Liberia. Their language is also called Mende. One well-known Mende prince was Cinque, the leader of the *Amistad* rebellion.

✥ MIDDLE PASSAGE   Term coined to define sea voyage carrying slaves from West Africa to European colonies in America; was actually the second or "middle part" of the voyage from Europe to Africa to

the Americas and back to Europe. The term has come to be synonymous with cruel and inhuman packing of Africans on board ships
bound for America.

❖ MNEMONIC DEVICE   A device created to aid or stimulate
memory.

❖ NKISI/MINKISI   Singular and plural Bakongo words for charm
used for healing.

❖ NSIBIDI   Ideographic writing system of the Ejagham people of
Nigeria seen inscribed on buildings and body and in ground paintings.

❖ ON POINT   The term "on point" refers to the pattern block that
is rotated so that it rests on one of its four corners (points).

❖ ORAL HISTORY   A means of maintaining cultural history and
traditions in prewriting civilizations whereby memory and verbal passing
down of information verbally is essential. Often the information takes
"story" form.

❖ PATCHWORK   The word "patchwork" is often used as an um-
brella term covering several quiltmaking techniques. The proper use of
the word defines the method of joining pieces of contrasting fabric edge-
to-edge in creating a geometric design. Sometimes the patches of fabric
are irregular in shape and the resulting configuration is abstract and can
be improvisational. Often, "utilitarian quilts," those made quickly to provide immediate cover from the cold of winter, are improvisational in
design.

❖ PIECING   This term is synonymous with patchwork. Often the word is incorrectly used to include the appliqué method of quilt top construction. On occasion the term "piecing" is used metaphorically, indicating a joining or coming together of disparate elements. An example of this is piecing together a community of people whose ethnic, religious, and/or career backgrounds differ.

❖ PLANTATION GRAPEVINE   Communication system developed by slaves to pass information from one plantation to another without being detected by plantation owners or overseers.

❖ PORO   Men's secret society found throughout West Africa, but particularly strong in Sierra Leone among the Mende people.

❖ PRINCE HALL   Highly respected free black at time of American Revolution committed to aiding his enslaved brethren; to that end he was founder of first black Masonic Lodge, which later became named for him; today black Masons are known as Prince Hall Masons.

❖ QUILT KNOT   The quilt knot is a small knot placed at the end of a length of sturdy thread. This knot is gently pulled into the batting at the beginning of a row of quilting stitches. The knot makes a characteristic popping sound when pulled into the batting. Just prior to ending a row of quilt stitches, another knot is made and popped into the batting. These knots secure the row of stitches. Tradition dictates that the quilt knot is never visible on the quilt top or back. If this knot can be seen, it is considered a breech of quiltmaking etiquette and a sign of sloppy work.

❖ QUILT TOP   The quilt top is the top layer of the "quilt sandwich." The other two layers are the batting (usually a sheet of fluffy cotton or wool, an old blanket, old clothing, or an old tattered quilt) and the backing (fabric sewn together to make a solid cloth sheet).

❖ QUILTING   The word "quilting" refers to the binding together of the quilt top, the quilt batting, and the quilt backing, employing small regular or large irregular stitches. The quilting also adds dimension to the overall quilt design. Traditionally, the quilting stitches accent, embellish, or complement the quilt top design.

❖ RING RITUAL/RING SHOUT   African ritual incorporating dance, drum, and song; transported to America, where heels are pounded on the floor to create the rhythm that drums used to pound out. Participants formed a circle and moved in a dance-like manner counterclockwise, being careful not to cross their feet. This ritual formed a "prayer dance," fostering community solidarity. Often dancers would enter a trance-like state.

❖ SANDE   Women's secret society found throughout West Africa. Its purpose was to prepare young women for their role in the community.

❖ SHANGO   Yoruba god of thunder and lightning; symbolized by colors red and white.

❖ TYING OR TACKING   To tie or to tack a quilt is to bind all three layers together using heavy thread, twine, cord, or yarn. A large needle threaded with the yarn or other strong material is pushed down through the three layers and pushed up. The yarn or cord is then knotted on the quilt surface and cut, forming what looks like a little tail. These ties are positioned about every two to four inches apart. This technique secures the layers together in a quick and easy manner while imparting a rustic appearance. Ties are frequently used when the batting of the quilt is thick and heavy. Ties are also favored in quilt construction when time is the determining factor.

❖ UKARA CLOTH   A combination of geometric and figurative designs in a dark color on a light background, made by Igbo people of Nigeria; cloth belongs to the Leopard Society.

❖ VAI   A syllabary instead of an alphabetic system of writing seen in West Africa among the Vai people of Sierra Leone and Liberia. This pictographic form of writing is believed to date from the seventeenth century.

Bibliography

Adams, Janus. *Escape to Freedom: Underground Railroad*. Back Pax International Ltd., 1988.

Aherne, Tavy D. *Nakunte Diarra: Bogolanfini Artist of the Beledougou*. Bloomington, Indiana: Indiana University Art Museum, 1992.

Allen, William Francis, Charles Picard Ware, and Lucy McKim Garrison. *Slave Songs of the United States*. Bedford, Massachusetts, 1867.

Bebey, Francis. *African Music: A People's Art*. Translated by Josephine Bennet. New York: Lawrence Hill Books, 1975.

Beers, Leland. *Towpath Topsy: Stories of the Ohio Canal at Dresden*. San Francisco: Proctor Jones Publishing Company, 1994.

Benberry, Cuesta. "A Quilt Research Surprise." *Quilter's Newsletter Magazine*, July/August 1981.

—————. *Always There: The African-American Presence in American Quilts*. Kentucky: Kentucky Quilt Project, 1992.

Bender, Sue. *Plain and Simple: A Woman's Journey to the Amish*. New York: HarperCollins Publishers, 1989.

Blassinghame, John W. *The Slave Community: Plantation Life in the Antebellum South*. New York: Oxford University Press, 1973.

—————. ed. *Slave Testimony: Two Centuries of Letters, Speeches, Interviews, and Autobiographies*. Baton Rouge, Louisiana: Louisiana State University Press, 1977.

Blockson, Charles L. *The Hippocrene Guide to the Underground Railroad*. New York: Hippocrene Books, 1994.

—————. *The Underground Railroad*. New York: Berkley Books, 1987.

Bolster, W. Jeffrey. *Black Jacks: African American Seamen in the Age of Sail*. Cambridge, Massachusetts: Harvard University Press, 1997.

Boone, Sylvia Ardyn. *Radiance from the Waters: Ideals of Feminine Beauty in Mende Art*. New Haven, Connecticut: Yale University Press, 1986.

Bovill, Edward William, with introduction by Robert O. Collins. *The Golden Trade of the Moors: West African Kingdoms in the Fourteenth Century*. Princeton, New Jersey: Markus Wiener Publishers, 1995.

Brackman, Barbara. *Clues in the Calico: A Guide to Identifying and Dating Antique Quilts*. McLean, Virginia: EPM Publications, Inc., 1989.

——————. *Encyclopedia of Appliqué: An Illustrated, Numerical Index to Traditional and Modern Patterns.* McLean, Virginia: EPM Publications, Inc., 1993.

——————. *Encyclopedia of Pieced Quilt Patterns.* American Quilter's Society, 1993. Originally published, Kansas: Prairie Flower Publishing, 1979, 1984.

——————. *Quilts from the Civil War.* Concord, California: C&T Publishing, 1997.

Bradford, Sarah H. *Scenes in the Life of Harriet Tubman.* Salem, New Hampshire: Ayer Company, Publishers, Inc., 1992. Originally published, Auburn, New York: W. J. Moses, Printer, 1869.

——————, 2nd ed., 1886, with introduction by Butler A. Jones. *Harriet Tubman: The Moses of Her People.* Gloucester, Massachusetts: Peter Smith Publisher, 1981 (reprints of current books 1961).

Branch, Muriel Miller. *The Water Brought Us: The Story of the Gullah-Speaking People.* New York: Cobblehill Books/Dutton, 1995.

Buckmaster, Henrietta. *Flight to Freedom: The Story of the Underground Railroad.* New York: Thomas Y. Crowell Company, 1958.

Burnside, Madeleine, and Rosemarie Robotham. *Spirits of the Passage: The Transatlantic Slave Trade in the Seventeenth Century.* New York: Simon and Schuster, 1997.

Butt-Thompson, F. W. *West African Secret Societies: Their Organizations, Officials and Teachings.* New York: Argosy-Antiquarian Ltd., 1969. Originally published, Sentry Press, 1929.

Campbell, Edward D. C., Jr., ed. *Before Freedom Came: African-American Life in the Antebellum South*. Exhibition catalog. Richmond, Virginia: Museum of the Confederacy and University of Virginia Press, 1919.

Cannizzo, Jeanne. *Into the Heart of Africa*. Exhibition catalog. Toronto: Royal Ontario Museum, 1989.

Carawan, Guy, and Candie Carawan, eds. *Ain't You Got a Right to the Tree of Life: The People of Johns Island, South Carolina—Their Faces, Their Words, and Their Songs*. Athens and London, Georgia: University of Georgia Press, 1966.

Child, Lydia Maria. *Isaac T. Hopper*. Boston: J. P. Jewett and Company, 1853.

Clark, Ricky. *Quilts and Carousels: Folk Art in the Firelands*. Oberlin, Ohio: Firelands Association for the Visual Arts, 1983.

Coffin, Levi. *Reminiscences*. Cincinnati: Robert Clark and Company, 1876.

Cohen, Anthony. *The Underground Railroad in Montgomery County, Maryland*. Montgomery County Historical Society, 1995.

Cooper, Patricia, and Norma Bradley Allen. *The Quilters: Women and Domestic Art*. New York: Anchor Press/Doubleday, 1978.

Cornelius, Janet Duitsman. *When I Can Read My Title Clear: Literacy, Slavery, and Religion in the Antebellum South*. University of South Carolina Press, 1991.

Courlander, Harold. *Negro Folk Music, U.S.A.* New York: Dover Publications, 1992. Originally published, Columbia University Press, 1963.

Creel, Margaret Washington. *A Peculiar People: Slave Religion and Community-Culture Among the Gullahs.* New York and London: New York University Press, 1988.

Cross, Mary Bywater. *Quilts and Women of the Mormon Migrations.* Nashville, Tennessee: Rutledge Hill Press, 1996.

—————. *Treasures in the Trunk: Quilts of the Oregon Trail.* Nashville, Tennessee: Rutledge Hill Press, 1993.

Curtin, Philip, Steven Feireman, Leonard Thompson, and Jan Vansina. *African History: From Earliest Times to Independence.* London and New York: Longman, 1995.

Diamond, Arthur. *Prince Hall: Social Reformer.* Chelsea House Publishers, 1992.

Dobard, Raymond G. "A Covenant in Cloth: The Visible and the Tangible in African-American Quilts." *Connecting Stitches: Quilts in Illinois Life.* Symposium papers, edited by Janice Tauer Wass. Springfield, Illinois: Illinois State Museum, 1995.

—————. "Quilts as Communal Emblems and Personal Icons." *The International Review of African American Art,* vol. 11, no. 2 (1994). Hampton, Virginia: Hampton University Museum.

Dobie, J. Frank. *Foller de Drinkin' Gou'd.* Austin, Texas: Texas Folklore Society, 1928.

Douglass, Frederick. *The Life and Times of Frederick Douglass.* New York: Collier Books, 1962. Originally published 1892.

—————. *My Bondage and My Freedom.* New York: Arno Press, 1968. Originally published 1855.

————————. *Narrative of the Life of Frederick Douglass*. Boston: American Anti-Slavery Society, 1845.

Du Bois, W. E. B., with introduction by Edgar Wideman. *The Souls of Black Folk*. New York: Vintage Books, 1990.

Elish, Dan. *Harriet Tubman and the Underground Railroad*. Gateway Civil Rights/The Millbrook Press, 1993.

Epstein, Dena J. *Sinful Tunes and Spirituals: Black Folk Music to the Civil War*. Urbana and Chicago: University of Illinois Press, 1977.

Everette, Susanne. *History of Slavery*. New Jersey: Chartwell Books Ltd., 1996.

Ferrero, Pat, Elaine Hedges, and Julie Silber. *Hearts and Hands: The Influence of Women and Quilts on American Society*. San Francisco: Quilt Digest Press, 1987.

Finley, Ruth E. *Old Patchwork Quilts and the Women Who Made Them*. Newton Center, Massachusetts: Charles T. Brandford Company, 1929. Reprint, McLean, Virginia: EPM Publications, 1992.

Fisher, Miles Mark. *Negro Slave Songs in the United States*. New York: Citadel Press, 1968. Originally published 1953.

Floyd, Samuel A., Jr. *The Power of Black Music*. New York and Oxford: Oxford University Press, 1995.

Forde, Daryll, ed. *African Worlds: Studies in the Cosmological Ideas and Social Values of African Peoples*. London, New York, and Toronto: Oxford University Press, 1954.

Foster, Helen Bradley. *New Raiments of Self: African American Clothing in the Antebellum South*. Berg: Oxford International Publishers, 1997.

Fox, Sandi. "The Log Cabin: An American Quilt on the Western Frontier." *The Quilt Digest 1*, San Francisco: Quilt Digest Press, 1985.

Franklin, John Hope. *From Slavery to Freedom*. New York: Alfred A. Knopf, 1967.

Freeman, Roland L. *A Communion of the Spirits: African-American Quilters, Preservers, and Their Stories*. Nashville, Tennessee: Rutledge Hill Press, 1996.

Fry, Gladys-Marie. "Harriet Powers: Portrait of a Black Quilter." *Missing Pieces: Georgia Folk Art 1770–1976*. Edited by Anna Wadsworth. Atlanta: Georgia Council of the Arts and Humanities, 1976.

————. *Stitched from the Soul: Slave Quilts from the Ante-Bellum South*. New York: Dutton Books, 1990.

Frye, L. Thomas, ed. *American Quilts: A Handmade Legacy*. Exhibition catalog. Oakland, California: Oakland Museum, 1981.

Gara, Larry. *The Liberty Line: The Legend of the Underground Railroad*. Lexington, Kentucky: University of Kentucky Press, 1961.

Gates, Henry Louis, Jr., and Nellie Y. McKay. *The Norton Anthology of African American Literature*. W. W. Norton and Company, 1997.

Genovese, Eugene D. *Roll Jordan Roll: The World the Slave Made*. New York: Pantheon Books, 1974.

Georgia Writers' Project. *Drums and Shadows: Survival Studies Among the Georgia Coastal Negroes*, 1940.

Gorrell, Gena K. *North Star to Freedom*. New York: Delacorte Press, 1996.

Goss, Linda, and Clay Goss. *Jump Up and Say: A Collection of Black Storytelling*. New York: Simon and Schuster, 1995.

Grudin, Eva Ungar. *Stitching Memories: African-American Story Quilts*. Williamstown, Massachusetts: Williams College Museum of Art, 1990.

Hall, Carrie A., and Rose G. Kretsinger. *The Romance of the Patchwork Quilt in America*. Caldwell, Idaho: Caxton Printers, 1935.

Hamilton, Virginia. *Many Thousand Gone: African-Americans from Slavery to Freedom*. New York: Alfred A. Knopf, 1993.

——————. *The People Could Fly: American Black Folktales*. New York: Alfred A. Knopf, 1985.

Harding, Vincent. *There Is a River: The Black Struggle for Freedom in America*. New York: Harvest Books/Harcourt Brace and Company, 1981.

Haskins, Jim. *Get on Board: The Story of the Underground Railroad*. New York: Scholastic Inc., 1993.

Herr, Patricia T. "Quaker Quilts and Their Makers." *Pieced by Mother: Symposium Papers*. Edited by Jeannette Lasansky. Pennsylvania: Oral Traditions Project, University of Pennsylvania Press, 1988.

Holloway, Joseph E. *Africanisms in American Culture*. Bloomington, Indiana: Indiana University Press, 1990.

Holstein, Jonathan, and John Finley. *Kentucky Quilts 1800–1900*. New York: Pantheon Books, 1982.

Hopkinson, Deborah. *Sweet Clara and the Freedom Quilt*. New York: Alfred A. Knopf, 1993.

Horton, James Oliver. *Free People of Color: Inside the African American*

Community. Washington, D.C., and London: Smithsonian Institution Press, 1993.

Howell, Donna Wyant, ed. Chapter One, "Descriptions of Plantation Life," and Chapter Three, "The Lives of Women." In *I Was a Slave: True Life Stories Told by Former American Slaves in the 1930's.* Washington, D.C.: American Legacy T.M. Books, 1997.

Hufford, Mary, Marjorie Hunt, and Steven Zeitlin. *The Grand Generation: Memory, Mastery, Legacy.* Smithsonian Institution Press, 1987.

Hurmence, Belinda, ed. *Before Freedom: When I Just Can Remember.* Winston-Salem, North Carolina: John F. Blair, Publisher, 1989.

Jeffries, Rosalind. "African Retentions in African American Quilts and Artifacts." *The International Review of African American Art.* Hampton, Virginia: Hampton University Press, 1994.

Johnson, James Weldon, and J. Rosamond Johnson. *American Negro Spirituals.* New York: Da Capo Press, 1969. Originally published 1925 and 1926 as two volumes.

Johnson, Paul E., ed. *African American Christianity: Essays in History.* Berkeley, Los Angeles, and London: University of California Press, 1994.

Jones, Arthur C. *Wade in the Water: The Wisdom of the Spirituals.* Maryknoll, New York: Orbis Books, 1993.

Jones, G. I. *Ibo Art.* Great Britain: Shire Publications Ltd. and C. I. Thomas and Sons, 1989.

Journal of the Senate of Virginia, 1831, pp. 9–10.

Kiewe, H. E. "Can Migration of Man Be Traced by African Textile Designs?" *West Africa Magazine,* June 25, 1955.

214   Hidden in Plain View

Kiracofe, Roderick, and Mary Johnson. *The American Quilt: A History of Cloth and Comfort 1750–1950*. New York: Clarkson Potter Publishers, 1993.

Larymore, Constance. *A Residence's Wife in Nigeria*. London: George Routledge and Sons Ltd., 1908; New York: E. P. Dutton, 1908.

Lasansky, Jeannette, ed. *In the Heart of Pennsylvania*. Symposium papers. Lewisburg, Pennsylvania: Oral Traditions Project, 1986.

—————, ed. *On the Cutting Edge: Textile Collectors, Collections, and Traditions*. Lewisburg, Pennsylvania: Oral Traditions Project, 1994.

—————, ed. *Pieced by Mother*. Symposium papers. Lewisburg, Pennsylvania: Oral Traditions Project, 1988.

Leon, Eli. *Who'd a Thought It: Improvisation in African-American Quiltmaking*. San Francisco: Craft and Folk Art Museum, 1987.

—————. *Models in the Mind: African Prototypes in American Patchwork*. Diggs Gallery, Winston-Salem State University, Winston-Salem, North Carolina, 1992.

Lewis, Samella, and Juliette Bowles. *The International Review of African American Art*, vol. 11, no. 2 (1994). Hampton, Virginia: Hampton University Press.

Litwack, Leon, and August Meier. *Black Leaders of the Nineteenth Century*. University of Illinois Press, 1988.

Logan, Paul, ed. *A Howard Reader: An Intellectual and Cultural Quilt of the African-American Experience*. Boston, Massachusetts: Houghton Mifflin, 1997.

Lohrenz, Mary Edna, and Anita Miller Stamper. *Mississippi Homespun:*

Nineteenth-Century Textiles and the Women Who Made Them. Mississippi State Historical Museum, 1989.

Longaberger, Glenn. *Dresden—1817–1967: Pioneer Days to Modern Ways.* Dresden, Ohio: Lindsey Printing Service, 1967 and 1991.

Lovell, John. *Black Song: The Forge and the Flame.* New York: Macmillan, 1972.

Lyons, Mary E. *Stitching Stars: The Story Quilts of Harriet Powers.* New York: Charles Scribner's Sons, 1993.

MacDowell, Marsha L., and C. Kurt Dewhurst, eds. *To Honor and Comfort: Native Quilting Traditions.* Museum of New Mexico Press, 1997.

Mack, John. *Emil Torday and the Art of the Congo: 1900–1909.* Seattle, Washington: University of Washington Press, 1990.

Mackey, Albert Gallatin. *The History of Freemasonry: Symbolism of Freemasonry; the Ancient and Accepted Scottish Rite and the Royal Order of Scotland; Addenda.* New York and London: Masonic History Company, 1906. Originally published 1898.

Mashuta, Mary. *Story Quilts: Telling Your Tale in Fabric.* C&T Publishing, 1992.

McLaurin, Melton A. *Celia, a Slave.* New York: Avon Books, 1991.

McNaughton, Patrick R. *The Mande Blacksmiths: Knowledge, Power, and Art in West Africa.* Bloomington, Indiana: Indiana University Press, 1988.

Mintz, Sidney W., and Richard Price. *The Birth of the African-American Culture.* Boston: Beacon Press, 1976.

Morris, Jean, and Eleanor Preston-Whyte. *Speaking with Beads: Zulu Arts from Southern Africa.* Thames and Hudson, 1994.

Murie, James R. *Ceremonies of the Pawnee*. Lincoln, Nebraska: University of Nebraska Press, 1981.

Nooter, Mary H., ed. *Secrecy: African Art That Conceals and Reveals*. New York: Museum of African Art, 1993.

Nzegwu, Nkiru, and Barbara Glass, eds. *Uncommon Beauty in Common Objects: The Legacy of African American Craft Art*. Wilberforce, Ohio: National Afro-American Museum and Cultural Center, 1993.

Oliver, Roland, and J. D. Fage. *A Short History of Africa*. New York: Penguin Books, 1995.

Orlofsky, Patsy, and Myron Orlofsky. *Quilts in America*. New York: McGraw-Hill Book Company, 1974.

Parrish, Lydia. *Slave Songs of the Georgia Sea Islands*. Athens, Georgia: University of Georgia Press, 1942.

Pazant, Rosalie F. *Never Too Late: The Life and Times of a Gullah Woman*. South Carolina: Pazant, 1992.

Perry, Regenia A. *Harriet Powers's Bible Quilts*. Rizzoli Art Series/St. Martin's Press, 1994.

Pesci, David. *Amistad: A Novel*. New York: Marlowe and Company, 1997.

Picton, John, and John Mack. *African Textiles*. New York: Harper and Row, Publishers, 1989.

Pinkney, Andrea Davis. *Dear Benjamin Banneker*. New York: Gulliver Books/Harcourt Brace and Company, 1994.

Plumer, Cheryl. *African Textiles*. East Lansing, Michigan: Michigan State University, 1971.

Potkay, Adam, and Sandra Burr. *Black Writers of the 18th Century.* New York: St. Martin's Press, 1995.

Powers, Bernard E., Jr. *Black Charlestonians: A Social History, 1822–1885.* Fayetteville, Arkansas: University of Arkansas Press, 1994.

Price, Ricard. *Maroon Societies: Rebel Slave Communities in the Americas.* Baltimore, Maryland: Johns Hopkins University Press, 1979.

Proctor, Samuel DeWitt. *The Substance of Things Hoped For: A Memoir of African American Faith.* New York: G. P. Putnam's Sons, 1995.

Quarles, Benjamin. *Black Abolitionists.* New York: Oxford University Press, 1969.

———. *The Negro in the Making of America.* New York: Simon and Schuster, 1987.

Rampersad, Arnold, ed. *The Collected Poems of Langston Hughes.* New York: Vintage Classics, 1995.

Ringgold, Faith. *Aunt Harriet's Underground Railroad in the Sky.* New York: Dragonfly Books/Crown Publishers, 1992.

Roan, Nancy, and Donald Roan. *Lest I Shall Be Forgotten: Anecdotes and Traditions of Quilts.* Green Lane, Pennsylvania: Goschenhoppen Historians, Inc., 1993.

Roberts, Mary Nooter, and Allen F. Roberts. *Memory: Luba Art and the Making of History.* Exhibition catalog. New York: Museum of African Art. Smithsonian Institution, 1996.

Ross, Alexander M. *Recollections and Experiences of an Abolitionist.* Toronto: Rowell and Hutchinson, 1875.

Segy, Ladislas. *Masks of Black Africa*. New York: Dover Publications, 1976.

Sieber, Roy, and Roslyn Adele Walker. *African Art in the Cycle of Life*. Washington, D.C., and London: Smithsonian Institution Press, 1987.

Siebert, Wilbur. *The Beginnings of the Underground Railroad in Ohio*. Ohio, 1898.

—————. *The Underground Railroad: From Slavery to Freedom*. New York: Macmillan Company, 1898.

Smedley, Robert C. *History of the Underground Railroad in Chester and the Neighboring Counties of Pennsylvania*. Lancaster, Pennsylvania: Office of the Journal, 1883.

Sobel, Mechal. *Trabelin' On: The Slave Journey to an Afro-Baptist Faith*. Princeton, New Jersey: Princeton University Press, 1988. Originally published, Greenwood Press, 1979.

Still, William. *The Underground Railroad*. Chicago: Johnson Publishing, 1970. Originally published 1871.

Strother, Horatio T. *The Underground Railroad in Connecticut*. Middletown, Connecticut: Wesleyan University Press, 1962.

Temple, Robert K. G. *The Sirius Mystery*. Rochester, Vermont: Destiny Books, 1987.

Thompson, Robert Farris. *Flash of the Spirit: African and Afro-American Art and Philosophy*. New York: Vintage Books/Random House, 1984.

Van Sertima, Ivan. *They Came Before Columbus: The African Presence in Ancient America*. New York: Random House, 1976.

Ventura, Michael. "Hear That Long Snake Moan." *Whole Earth Review*, no. 54 (spring 1987).

————. "Hear That Long Snake Moan," Part II. *Whole Earth Review*, no. 55 (summer 1987).

Vlach, John Michael. *Back of the Big House: The Architecture of Plantation Slavery*. University of North Carolina Press, 1993.

————. *Charleston Blacksmith: The Work of Philip Simmons*. University of South Carolina Press, 1992.

Voorhis, Harold Van Buren. *Negro Masonry in the United States*. Kila, Montana: Kessinger Publishing Company, 1939.

Wahlman, Maude Southwell. *Signs and Symbols: African Images in African-American Quilts*. New York: Studio Books, in association with Museum of American Folk Art, 1993.

Walkes, Joseph A., Jr. *Black Square and Compass: 200 Years of Prince Hall Freemasonry*. Richmond, Virginia: Macoy Publishing and Masonic Supply Company, 1979.

————. *A Prince Hall Masonic Quiz Book*. Richmond, Virginia: Macoy Publishing and Masonic Supply Company, 1989.

Wardlaw, Alvia, et al. *Black Art Ancestral Legacy: The African Impulse in African-American Art*. Dallas, Texas: Hurst Printing Company/Abrams. Dallas Museum of Art, 1989.

Willis, Bruce W. *The Adinkra Dictionary: A Visual Primer on the Language of ADINKRA*. Washington, D.C.: The Pyramid Complex, 1998.

Wilson, Harriet E. *Our Nig: Or, Sketches from the Life of a Free Black*. New York: Random House, 1985.

Wilson, Sule Greg. *The Drummer's Path: Moving the Spirit with Ritual and Traditional Drumming.* Rochester, Vermont: Destiny Books, 1992.

Winter, Jeanette. *Follow the Drinking Gourd.* New York: Dragonfly Books/Alfred A. Knopf, 1988.

Wright, Courtney C. *Journey to Freedom: A Story of the Underground Railroad.* New York: Holiday House, 1994.